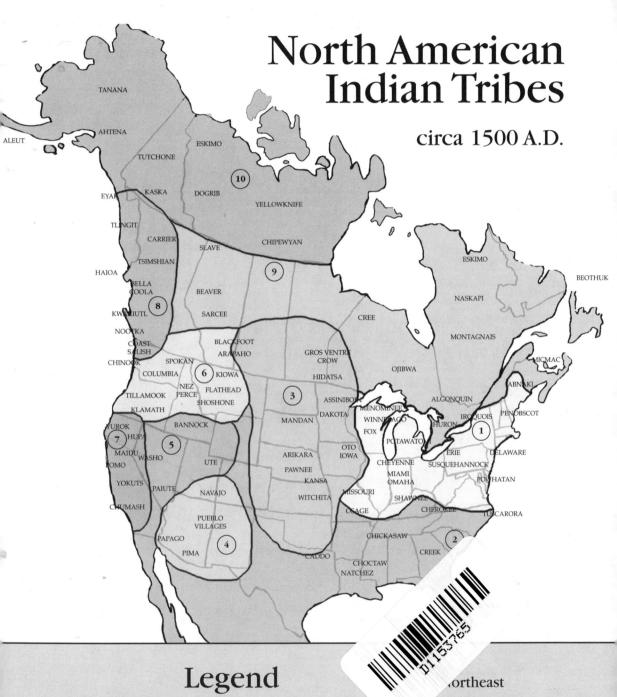

North American Indian Tribes

circa 1500 A.D.

ALEUT
TANANA
AHTENA
ESKIMO
TUTCHONE
EYAK
KASKA
DOGRIB
(10)
YELLOWKNIFE
TLINGIT
CARRIER
SLAVE
CHIPEWYAN
ESKIMO
BEOTHUK
TSIMSHIAN
HAIOA
(9)
BELLA COOLA
BEAVER
NASKAPI
(8)
KWAKIUTL
SARCEE
CREE
MONTAGNAIS
NOOTKA
BLACKFOOT
COAST SALISH
ARAPAHO
GROS VENTRE
CROW
OJIBWA
MICMAC
CHINOOK
SPOKAN
COLUMBIA
(6)
KIOWA
HIDATSA
ABNAKI
TILLAMOOK
NEZ PERCE
FLATHEAD
SHOSHONE
(3)
ASSINIBOIN
DAKOTA
MENOMINEE
WINNEBAGO
ALGONQUIN
HURON
IROQUOIS
PENOBSCOT
(1)
KLAMATH
MANDAN
FOX
POTAWATOMI
ERIE
DELAWARE
YUROK
(7)
HUPA
BANNOCK
(5)
WASHO
UTE
ARIKARA
PAWNEE
KANSA
OTO
IOWA
CHEYENNE
MIAMI
OMAHA
SUSQUEHANNOCK
POWHATAN
MAIDU
POMO
YOKUTS
PAIUTE
NAVAJO
WITCHITA
MISSOURI
OSAGE
SHAWNEE
CHEROKEE
TUSCARORA
CHUMASH
PUEBLO VILLAGES
PAPAGO
PIMA
(4)
CADDO
CHICKASAW
CREEK
(2)
CHOCTAW
NATCHEZ

Legend

		1 - Northeast
2 - Southeast	3 - Plains	4 - Southwest
5 - Great Basin	6 - Plateau	7 - California
8 - Northwest Coast	9 - Subarctic	10 - Arctic

MY LODGE

SIMPLE WAS MY LODGE
OF BIRCH

PURE WAS THE WATER
THAT I DRANK

SWIFT WAS THE CANOE
THAT CARRIED ME

STRAIGHT WAS THE ARROW
THAT PROTECTED ME

WILD WAS THE MEAT
THAT FED ME

SWEET WAS THE
SUGAR MAPLE

STRONG WERE THE HERBS
THAT SUSTAINED ME

GREAT WAS MY MOTHER
THE EARTH

DUKE REDBIRD
Native Poet, Ontario , Canada

NATIVE INDIAN WILD GAME, FISH & WILD FOODS COOKBOOK

RECIPES FROM NORTH AMERICAN
NATIVE COOKS

EDITED BY DAVID HUNT

FOX BOOKS

Fox Chapel Publishing Co Inc.

Fox Chapel Publishing
Box 7948 - W
Lancaster, Pennsylvania
USA 17604

THE NATIVE INDIAN WILD GAME, FISH AND WILD FOODS COOKBOOK

©1992, 1997, Fox Chapel Publishing Company,
all rights reserved

Publisher: Alan Giagnocavo
Cover Design: Tom Robbins
Research: Steve Palme
Indexing: Louise Stoltzfus
Layout: Chuck Golding

This is an newly revised and typeset Second Edition of a book of the same title first published in 1992

Manufactured in the United States of America

To order additional copies of this book,
please send $14.95 plus $2.50 postage to:

Fox Chapel Book Orders
Box 7948
Lancaster, Pennsylvania 17604

Please try your bookstore first!

TABLE OF CONTENTS

FOREWORD

This very special book will introduce you to the foods of North American Native peoples.

The recipes, information and artwork represents a collaborative effort with various native groups to bring together in one comprehensive, practical reference the unique taste and history of this cooking that is so closely linked to a dependence on the land and nature.

To the best of my knowledge, our project is the only one of its kind - the only book on Native cookery written by Native people themselves. After conceiving of this idea for a book, we contacted numerous Native groups across North America. Certain tribes could provide us with little or no information. In other cases we were very fortunate in unearthing a treasure trove of recipes and lore. Special thanks are due to Brenda Anstey and Beverly Brown of the Lovesick Lake Native Women's Association. The research and information they gathered from an extensive two year oral history project formed the backbone for this book. Less extensive, but no less important, are the collections we received from the Cherokee in North Carolina, groups in the Southwest and in the Pacific Northwest.

Although this project was produced in-house, early on we decided to donate 100% of the royalties that would normally be paid to an author to Native charities. So far, the $1000's of dollars in royalties earned from your purchases of this book have gone to worthwhile projects such as: college scholarships for young native women, an Ojibway children's camp and substance abuse programs among Native peoples.

I find all of our publications fascinating to work on, but this project has been an exceptionally interesting one. I'm sure you'll find yourself spending hours in reading and cooking from these pages.

ALAN GIAGNOCAVO
Publisher

SUGGESTED MENUS FOR SPECIAL DINNERS

MENU 1

Curried Rabbit (p. 65) with Wild Cranberry Conserve (p. 185)
Glazed Milkweed Stalks (p. 167)
Baked Turnips (p. 176)
Acorn Bread (p. 192)
Plains Indian Dessert (p. 192)

MENU 2

Sorrel Soup (p. 172)
Baked Sea Bass with Chestnuts (p. 126)
Baked Wild Rice and Carrots (p. 149)
Strawberries and Honey Sauce (p. 190)

MENU 3

Cream of Fiddlehead Soup with Mushrooms (p. 165)
Blueberry Duck Roast (p. 86)
Baked Cucumbers (p. 178)
Adobe Bread (p. 171)
Huckleberry Crisp (p. 189)

MENU 4

Pinon Soup (p. 174)
Salmon with Watercress (p. 123)
Corny Morels (p. 167)
Gwap Giz Gun (p. 153)
Blueberry-Orange Loaf (p. 188)

LIGHTER MENUS FOR SPECIAL LUNCHES

MENU 5

Pumpkin Soup (p. 191)
Eggs and Wild Onions (p. 177)
Potato Scones (p. 154)
Baked Rhubarb and Strawberries (p. 190)

MENU 6

Chippewa Wild Rice (p. 149)
Huckleberry Muffins (p. 188)
Wild Applesauce (p. 185)

MENU 7

Moose and Cabbage Turnovers (p. 61)
Curried Fruit (p. 186)

A FESTIVE GET-TOGETHER FOR A CROWD

MENU 8

Oyster Soup (p. 174)
Chestnuts and Bacon (p. 195)
Sweet-and-Sour Venison Meatballs (p. 46)
Wild Goose with Apple and Raisin Stuffing (p. 92)
Catfish Bake (p. 133)
Dandelion Greens Supreme (p. 164)
Marinated Fiddleheads (p. 165)
Bean Cake (p. 178)
Bacon Cornbread (p. 153)

INTRODUCTION

For most people living in the United States today, the impression of Native Americans is that offered up in films and pulp fiction: the Plains horseman, wearing warpaint and fringed buckskin, tearing across the prairie, long braids blown back, his war whoop causing the young mothers to pull their children closer as he and his brothers ride after a wagon train firing arrows and waving tomahawks; the chief posed, regal and somber, with his ceremonial spear and long tobacco pipe, feathered war bonnet trailing down his back to brush the ground; the mystic in the desert, leaning close to a low fire and offering cryptic prophecies in halting English; the lone brave paddling his birchbark canoe down pristine waterways that curve through idyllic maple and oak forests. These simple images, while they may have occurred somewhere in history (there was, at some point in the last several thousand years, probably a Chippewa brave returning home one afternoon in his canoe down a woodland stream where the leaves had just transformed into brilliant red and gold), they offer a poor, one-dimensional view of the incredible number of diverse cultures and peoples lumped together under the terms "Native American" and "American Indian."

The recipes collected in this volume represent a cross-section of dozens of tribes from all across North America. Many are for traditional foods, the essential methods of preparation passed down through generations, while others are contemporary innovations that utilize ingredients not available even fifty or a hundred years ago. But this is still only a small part of the history and culture of the Native American people.

PRE-EUROPEAN AMERICA

Over thousands of years, since the first people crossed the Bering Strait land bridge during the last Ice Age, the original settlers of North America have adapted to inhabit nearly every portion of the continent, building complex societies and learning to use every aspect of their particular surroundings. They domesticated plants and animals, divided into hundreds of languages and dialects, and became protectors and utilizers of an entire continent. Throughout the diversity of these many tribes, there are a few essential traits that, while they may take on slightly different outward appearances from group to group, remain constant across all the various people who originally colonized America.

The most basic commonality of the Native American peoples was their relationship with the natural world. The environment was the deciding factor in the lifestyle of any particular group. Where game was plentiful, there were excellent hunters, if there was good soil, agriculture played a large role, areas with rivers and lakes or coastal waters meant fishermen, and harsher climates, like the Great Basin, were home to hunter-gatherers. No matter how tough it was to make a living for a tribe or a clan though, Nature was viewed not as an adversary, but as something which supported and nurtured the people; something powerful which commanded respect but, at the same time, needed to be cared for and protected. Among the tribes of the Southeast—the Cherokee, Creek, Tumucua, Choctaw and others—the animals were referred to as the "First People." Hunters would give special prayers of thanks and words of love and respect to the deer, rabbits and other game that gave up their lives to feed the villages. On the Plains the buffalo was the source of survival for all and the embodiment of the loving spirit of nature. Everything—every animal, tree, stream and stone—possessed a spirit. Both good and evil, these spirits were the game and the crops that sustained them, the cause and the cure of disease, the rains and snows that made for hard times in the villages. Collectively, they were called the "Great Spirit," the "Everything Spirit," *Wakonda*, *Wakan Tanka* and other names. It was part of the relationship the Native Americans had with nature; a World Soul of which they were a part, along with every blade of grass, smooth river pebble and quick-footed deer.

One of the most sacred gifts of the Earth was tobacco. It was a cure, used in medicines by many tribes for almost any ailment, a part of ritual songs and dances, the finishing touch on any pact or agreement and a symbol of friendship. In the spring, when tribes like the Delaware would settle into villages and plant crops along the coast of New Jersey, Delaware and Maryland, traders would range up and down the Eastern Seaboard, stopping at every village to mingle streams of smoke from their pipe with those of the villagers before any business was done. When the Sauk Fox of the Great Lakes held their ceremony of remembrance for the dead, the Ghost Dance, they would set out food, water and tobacco for the spirits of family members and friends who had passed on. Cherokee medicine men rubbed the leaves on stomachs of those with abdominal cramps, and some of the most sacred objects of the Sioux tribes were the five-foot, ornately carved calumets (pipes) that sealed peace agreements and confirmed intentions of war.

Corn, along with beans and squash, was a staple of most tribes and grown anywhere that the climate and the soil would allow. Even if corn could not be grown in a particular region, such as upper New England, it was traded for with skins, tobacco or anything else upon which a bargain could be struck. It was the traveling ration for hunting parties and warriors who would, at times, journey for days or weeks through the wild. Cherokee hunters took parched corn—a roasted and shelled preparation which is similar to hominy—as their only food source on long treks as they searched for game in the North Carolina woods. The war parties of the Iroquois carried corn meal and maple sugar which they would mix with water to make a high-carbohydrate high-sugar cereal as they journeyed to distant villages to exact revenge on their enemies. In the Southwest, one of the most difficult areas for Native people to eke out an existence, the tough-hulled blue corn would be pounded into a meal, then cooked with ash and spread on hot stone to make a traditional bread. It was an ingredient in nearly every soup and stew and sustained them through long winters. So important was this plant, which they had domesticated thousands of years earlier, that it had a sacred place in their myths and religious ceremonies. Many tribes, especially in the East and around the Great Lakes, celebrated the Green Corn Dance or, as it was often called, Busk. The ceremony was held at the time of the first harvest, usually late spring, and it was a festival of several days. It celebrated the renewal of life for the coming year through songs, dances, prayers, speeches, fasting and feasting. The first ripe ears of corn would be burned over a ceremonial fire and their ashes buried. A new fire was started and corn was cooked for the entire village to take part in the feast. The fire would be kept burning until the time of the next Green Corn Dance. On the Plains, tribes like the Pawnee would not begin the great buffalo hunts until the corn had been planted, and then they would return in time for harvest to celebrate before setting out again for the fall hunt, which could last for weeks. In the myths of the Cherokee and Choctaw, the "First Mother" or "Earth Mother," gave corn as a gift to mankind by sacrificing her own life. It sprang from her blood after she instructed her children to kill her. It was a symbol of the Earth's love for the people. In addition to being an almost universal food source, it was something which was constant throughout every aspect of an individual's life, from cradle to grave. Cornmeal compresses were used to soothe the umbilical cord of infants. Children played with dolls made of cobs or with hair of corn silk. The husks were used to make sleeping mats and weave baskets. Among the Cherokee, a ripe ear was given by a young girl to her suitor as a sign of acceptance of a marriage proposal. The cobs were used to scrub dirty children, and in rituals to honor the dead, it was cooked and set out to remember those who had passed on.

For thousands of years, the lives and traditions of the many tribes endured and evolved uninterrupted. They held their festivals, tended their crops, taught the boys to hunt and be warriors while the women tended children and, as with the Iroquois, directed the future of their clans. Life was not, however, the pure and idyllic commune with nature that many of the early Europeans reported after their first contact with the Native Americans. It was hard and unforgiving, even for those who had the benefit of fertile soil and abundant game in their territory. Metal was virtually nonexistent—arrowheads, spear points and cutting tools (such as knives used for skinning and dressing game) were made of stone. Their only domesticated animal was the dog, which although useful in many respects, made a poor pack animal and was nearly useless as a means of transport. This meant hunting large game, like buffalo and elk, was a grueling endeavor carried out entirely on foot. Complex strategies, often time consuming and requiring a large amount of manpower, had to be used. For nomadic and semi-nomadic people, moving their village from place to place as they followed the herds or moved to fresh hunting grounds meant every worldly possession had to be bundled up and loaded on the shoulders of the men, women, children and, in some cases, even the dogs. There the bundles remained for days as a clan trudged miles in search of a new territory. For many, living close to a waterway became essential as their canoes were the most effective means of transport they had at their disposal.

Warfare was another constant threat. Although large battles between tribes almost never occurred, there was a constant cycle of raids and vengeance—blood feuds between villages and tribes. Some groups were staunch pacifists and would not revenge themselves if raided, but the majority took part in these feuds. The Iroquois were literally bleeding themselves to death at one point in their history. Reputed for their tireless pursuit of vengeance and their ferocity in battle, the five tribes—Mohawk, Seneca, Onondaga, Cayuga and Oneida—almost completely destroyed themselves, much to the horror of council elders who complained that their hot-tempered young warriors raided and revenged themselves on everyone in range. It should be noted, however, that the concept of warfare for the Native Americans did not mean killing as many of the enemy as possible. Often greater personal glory was gained by some action of bravery, such as touching an enemy leader in battle, than killing a foe. This view of warfare had disastrous results when conflicts with the Europeans developed.

When Columbus arrived in the New World in 1492 he thought, mistakenly, that he had found the passage to the Orient and was sailing through the West Indies, so he called the natives "Indians." This initial misperception by Columbus, a man who also looked on these unusual people as a potential source of slave labor to be exploited, was a portent of things to come as the Europeans settled America.

THE NORTHEAST

At the beginning of the seventeenth century, the Northeast was thriving. The coastal tribes, like the Delaware and Powhatan, enjoyed the fertile coastal plains that stretched from Virginia well into New England. Good soil, abundant game, and some of the most fertile fishing waters to be found in the Atlantic offered more than enough for the tribes. Corn, squash, beans and pumpkins were grown on the flatlands. Fish were taken with nets or herded into enclosures using weirs, then speared. During the balmy days of summer, celebrations were held for the harvest of corn and strawberries. Traders would range from village to village bringing skins, tobacco, and stories with them. It was these tribes that encouraged the first Europeans settlers to send back reports of an innocent and gentle people living an Eden-like existence in the Americas.

Inland, the world became a vast, seemingly unending forest. In the green-filtered sunlight, beneath the canopy of birch, elm and oak, were the territories of the fierce woodland tribes—the League of the Iroquois. Living in what is now Upstate New York and along the coast of Lake Erie, the powerful alliance of the five Iroquois tribes was called by some the "Rome of the New World." Politically sophisticated, sedentary, and united in the most powerful tribal empire in North America, the Iroquois were a force with which to be reckoned. Almost all the tribes of the Northeast either warred with or paid homage to them and the Iroquois, in turn, lived up to both their peace agreements and their threats. The powerful League was the work of one man, a Mohawk named Hiawatha, who lived in the fourteenth century. A holy man, Dekanawidah, told him of a dream he had in which he saw the five nations united beneath the branches of the Great Tree of Peace. Hiawatha was deeply affected by the vision of Dekanawidah and set off in his canoe, traveling from village to village through the territory of the five nations of the Iroquois and urging them to set aside their feuds and unite with their Iroquois brothers. He succeeded at what seemed an impossible task and the council of the five nations was established. There were fifty seats on the council, but only forty-nine were occupied. No one was allowed to take Hiawatha's place on the council after his death—he was considered irreplaceable. The five nations themselves—Mohawk, Seneca, Oneida, Onondaga and Cayuga—each occupied their own strip of territory. They lived in longhouses and were ruled by the elder woman of each clan within the tribe. They did not have the huge herds of buffalo and elk to depend on and follow through the seasons like many of the western tribes. They made use of the forest, harvesting the sap of the maples, using acorns, sunflowers, apples, hunting the plentiful deer, bear and beaver and, of course, growing corn and tobacco.

Around the Iroquois lands were the more peaceful and numerous Algonquin tribes. It is they who are known for their birchbark canoes and wigwams. Ranging from the Great Lakes south to Virginia and Kentucky, the Algonquin people are believed to be the oldest inhabitants of the northeast and some of the first to come in contact and conflict with the European settlers. Their language is the source of over a hundred common English words like terrapin, succotash, hickory, woodchuck and moose.

Farther north, in what is now New Hampshire and Maine, lived semi-nomadic tribes such as the Micmac and Abnaki. With harsh terrain and bitter winters, the Micmac became some of the most accomplished hunters to be found anywhere in the East. On foot, or on snowshoes, they made their living off the moose. Very shy and solitary, the moose was difficult to hunt and every means possible was used to catch them; snares were set and birchbark moose calls used during the rutting season; hunters would dress in moose skins (antlers included) to get close enough for a bowshot; and in deep snow hunters would put on snowshoes and simply outrun them in the drifts. The moose supplied their clothes, furnished their wigwams (a temporary, dome-like shelter) and kept their stomachs full. Also important were the beaver and porcupine, which were hunted with dogs, and the abundant shellfish (freshwater and saltwater both) of the region. Corn and tobacco are not hardy enough to grow so far north though, and the Micmac and Abnaki were forced to trade with tribes living further south for them. This meant that, unlike many of the more southernly people, such as the Iroquois, Delaware and Cherokee, they had to make use of more roots, tubers and other wild plants that could be gathered and stored.

THE ARRIVAL OF THE EUROPEANS

The earliest European settlements were those of the English and the French. The English arrived first, at Jamestown, and quickly spread up the coast. It is from the Jamestown colony that what is now near legend, the story of Pocahontas and Captain John Smith, comes. The colonists arrived in 1607 and were faced with the terrible hardships of disease and starvation that, within a year, decimated their numbers. Powhatan, whose real name was Wah-hun-sen-a-cawh, was the chief of a loose confederacy of 32 Algonquin tribes—about 200 villages and 10,000 people. Initially, Powhatan permitted the colony to establish itself and even helped the starving settlers, showing them the use of some local plants and giving them what corn he could spare. Within a few years, the Jamestown settlement was thriving and new members were arriving from England in search of their fortunes. Tobacco quickly became a cash crop for the colonists but it was also a crop that exhausted the soil quickly and, by 1614, the colonists growing tobacco needed virgin soil. They found it easier to seize fields the Indians had already cleared than to clear new land. The conflict was inevitable. Powhatan tried to preserve an increasingly uneasy peace as petty squabbles became bloody and a cycle of revenge killings began. The Governor of Virginia, Sir Thomas Gates, was instructed to subjugate and make tributaries as many of the chiefs as possible and to kill the priests of the tribes. Instances of wholesale slaughter soon began. The Powhatan and other tribes along the James river began striking back, believing that failure to redress an injustice was not merciful, but an injustice in itself.

The colonists grew increasingly fearful, and more vicious, and the tribes quickly grew to mistrust the English and their bullying tactics. Pocahontas, the daughter of Powhatan, was kidnapped by one of the local Governors and used to barter with Powhatan for the return of captured colonists. During the year of her captivity, John Rolfe, a Calvinist, became enamored of her and courted her. Pocahontas agreed to marry him and her dowry was a promise of peace from Powhatan. The peace of Powhatan was short lived, however. It died with him and his brother, Opechancanough, became chief.

Opechancanough was not so enamored of the idea of peace with the English as his brother had been. He had already been held hostage once by Captain John Smith and had seen the brutal tactics of the colonists in action. The murder of an Algonquin who was employed by one of the colonists proved to be the last straw for Opechancanough. In 1622, he organized a synchronized attack along the length of the James river. The young warriors, who by that time were a common sight in and around the settlements and even worked within the homes of many English, at the agreed upon hour, attacked the colonists. The massacre, while it achieved Opechancanough's desired revenge, galvanized the colonists' view of the Native Americans as a threat to their existence that needed to be driven from their midst, using any means necessary.

The tribes, which included the Delaware, Powhatan and other coastal people, were brutalized, chiefs were taken hostage, and in one instance even poisoned, in an attempt to force them out. When the tribes retaliated by killing a number of colonists, entire villages were massacred by the settlers. There were some British officials, like Virginia Governor Sir William Berkely, who were horrified by the systematic destruction of the tribes, and did what they could to halt it, including issuing prohibitions against encroachment on tribal lands and arresting some of the colonists involved in particularly heinous acts against the Indians. The slightly more sympathetic officials were outnumbered, though, and more ruthless heads eventually prevailed, ousting or circumventing those who tried to protect the Native people. Eventually, their tribes all but destroyed, the remnants of the once thriving coastal people fled to the Ohio valley. It was a pattern destined to be repeated time and time again across America but, in the mid-seventeenth century, there was still an Eastern force to be contended with by the growing colonies. The westward push of the English was halted when they ran up against the power of the League of the Iroquois.

THE LEAGUE OF THE IROQUOIS

To the north, along the Canadian border and around the Great Lakes, the fur trade of the French was thriving. They took a much different approach to the local tribes than the English did, seeing them as an invaluable source of manpower and information that could be exploited. Tribes such as the Abnaki and the Huron helped the French, even supplying military aid to them during the French and Indian wars that began near the end of the seventeenth century. These tribes were not simply easily duped pawns of the French, though. While the war between the English and French may have seemed incomprehensible or even absurd to the Huron, Abnaki, Algonquin and Iroquois, there were motivations for these people that were well served by the alliances they chose. The Hurons gained weapons that finally gave them an advantage over the League of the Iroquois; the Abnaki needed arms and allies to fight the English and preserve their territory from both the colonists and the neighboring tribes. The Iroquois, surrounded by these enemies who had suddenly gained the upper hand in their age-old struggle and fighting French encroachment on their hard-won territory, found the English to be a valuable ally.

The League of the Iroquois was well organized, and they were an empire of warriors who knew the wild Appalachian forests better than any of the colonists. They were not so easily dispersed from their ancestral lands as the Delawares. The Huron, armed with French guns, exacted a heavy toll in their raids on the League, who still fought with bows and the traditional ironwood war clubs. The English, hoping to oust the French from their superior position in the northern fur trade and recognizing the disastrous consequences of an Iroquois-French alliance, courted the council of the League, offering them guns for their loyalty. The Iroquois happily lent their support and, now armed, went on the warpath against the Huron. In a few weeks, the well-armed League of the Iroquois slaughtered almost the entire Huron people. A nation of 30,000 was reduced to a few starving and terrified bands who fled west, eventually joining with what remained of the Delawares in the Ohio Valley. And the Iroquois, by the middle of the eighteenth century, had gained a hammerlock on the fur trade of the Northeast.

The loyalty of the Iroquois to their British allies would prove to be their undoing. With the coming of the American Revolution, the Iroquois sided with their old partners against the rebels. The defeat and withdrawal of the British at the end of the war spelled disaster for the League. They had made powerful enemies with the newly formed nation to their east, and no longer had an ally against the French to the north. Slowly, they began losing territory to the expansion of the United States. The Iroquois remained strong, however, and were still a force to be reckoned with until an enemy they had not anticipated appeared—smallpox.

Smallpox was a disease that had, in the past, ravaged Europe. Through the successive cycle of plagues, the Europeans had built a natural resistance to it. While still regarded as a terrible killer, they were not as vulnerable as someone who had never been exposed. The Iroquois, and every other people living in North America, had never been exposed to smallpox before. They also had not been exposed to a host of other flus, viruses and infections, like measles, which the Europeans brought with them. The consequences of this lack of resistance were terrible. A captain who sailed up the coast from the Carolinas to Massachusetts Bay said of the devastation, "It was as if I were witnessing a new found Golgotha." From an estimated population of sixteen million Native American people when the Spanish landed in the 1540s, only two million remained by the beginning of the eighteenth century, once the waves of disease had swept through their villages. It devastated the Iroquois. That, in combination with the ruthless tactics employed by the American Government to seize their lands, which included the wholesale slaughter of villages and the tearing out of crops, broke the power of the League of the Iroquois by the first half of the nineteenth century, and it would never recover.

THE SOUTHEAST

The tribes of the Southeast shared a fate similar to the tribes of New England and Virginia. The southern Gulf and Atlantic region was dominated by tribes like the Natchez, Choctaw, Creek, Cherokee and Timucua. They were hunters and farmers who enjoyed a more temperate climate, allowing them to remain more sedentary. Unlike the Algonquin and Iroquois tribes to the north, there was not such a prevalance of maple sugar in their diets. Instead, sarsaparilla, sassafras, wild berries—especially the strawberry—and other local plants were used to sweeten their meals. The hills of the Carolinas and Georgia were home to thousands of Cherokee who lived in villages, hunted deer and rabbits, tended their crops and trained their warriors with ball games, the most widely known of these being Lacrosse. The Cherokee version of Lacrosse was much more brutal than the modern sport, often resulting in the death of one or more of the participants. But they were training warriors, not playing simply for the sport of it.

The Timucuas occupied what is now Florida as well as much of the Carolina coast. They were fishermen, hunters and farmers who used the land with a reverence and expertise that was never achieved by the European settlers. Early settlers reported cornfields stretching for miles, ripening in the steamy Carolina summer while the Timucuas's young men played ball games on the courts in their villages or smoked the trophies of their hunts. One constant threat they faced was from alligators. Men were always on watch for them around the villages, and when one was seen or, more often, its loud bellowing was heard, they would hunt it down and kill it using a long pole. The pole was forced down the throat of the alligator, disabling its jaws, while several of the other hunters would flip it onto its back. At that point it was an easy task to dispatch the reptile with clubs. The meat could be smoked and the tough hide cured and used for any number of purposes.

To the west, in what is now Louisiana and southern Arkansas, lived the Choctaw, Creek and Natchez. In the low-lying forests and along the lower Mississippi, these tribes lived much as their eastern counterparts—growing corn, squash, beans and tobacco, fishing and hunting. The most respected of animals, for its swiftness and for what it provided in the way of food and clothing, was the deer. Prayers were offered to the spirits of their quarry—a rite to insure the rebirth of the animals and their continued availability to the people who depended on them. Hunting on foot through the heavy brush and marshlands, the people of the Southeastern tribes employed tactics similar to those the Abnaki and Micmac used when they pursued moose. Deerskins would be worn so that they could approach within easy bowshot; from boyhood animal calls were practiced so that, by the time the hunters were young men, they were masters at the various calls that could draw the game closer; group hunts would be organized where large numbers of hunters would set an area on fire, driving the deer before them and into the waiting bows of men concealed downwind of the burning brush.

These Southern tribes were not as quickly driven from their lands as many of the northern people, but they eventually succumbed to the advancing frontier as well.

EARLY CONTACT

First to be affected were the coastal people. In Spanish Florida, the Timucuas were ravaged by smallpox and measles during the seventeenth century, and suffered under the guns of the Spanish. By the time the English arrived, their numbers had been so reduced they posed little threat to those who would seize their lands. Caught between the Spanish, English, and hostile neighboring tribes, their numbers dwindled even further, and by the beginning of the eighteenth century, the Timucuas were a people known only in the reports and engravings of the early explorers. They had been slowly and inexorably exterminated by disease and sporadic conflict.

The Cherokee, Creek and Choctaw were larger tribes who could retreat far into the wild territory of the Smoky Mountains and the backwoods of Mississippi, Alabama and Louisiana. They suffered from outbreaks of smallpox and other imported illnesses that felled thousands of their people, but their land was not taken from them so readily. The colonists were not that numerous and there was no driving force to draw them into unknown territory in large numbers. The early settlers of the Southeast still managed to disrupt the lives of the Indians without seizing their lands by playing unscrupulously on any potential for profit. Liquor, guns and supplies were traded for skins, and it wasn't long before the hunters and warriors started trading with skins they didn't have. Working on promises of game they would catch in the coming months, many hunters were essentially enslaved by the debts they built up. There was also a very real slave trade in the Southeast. Mainly an English enterprise, it served several purposes. It spurred tribal warfare between groups who had strong trading ties with the English and those who were allied with the Spanish. Slavers would buy the prisoners of war that were captured in regular raids by Creeks and Cherokees on the people of Northern Florida. The slaves were often taken far from home to serve as field hands. It not only gave the colonists the manpower to clear large tracts of land, it emptied entire areas of their indigenous populations, making them available for the expanding settlers. By 1710, the northern Florida Peninsula was almost completely deserted.

There were uprisings against the colonists. Relations between the Creek and the British soured and, from time to time, they would organize attacks and slaughter a number of Europeans before disappearing into the hills. Expeditions were sent against the offending tribes, with orders for near-indiscriminate bloodshed as punishment, then new peace treaties would be signed. Sometimes the treaties would guarantee lands to the tribes. In a few months, or a few years, the colonists would move on to the protected land, begin farming it, and the cycle of rebellion and peace treaty would begin again, with the tribes gradually losing more and more ground.

THE RISE OF THE PLANTATIONS AND THE TRAIL OF TEARS

Eli Whitney and his invention, the cotton gin, revolutionized the processing of cotton. In the mid-eighteenth century, cotton was not a commercial crop in the South. Picking the seeds from the tangled blossoms was a long, tedious process that required too many slaves to make it profitable. The cotton gin could remove the seeds quickly and only a couple of slaves were needed to operate it. The southern plantation estate economy rose, built on the backs of Native American and African slaves and using the ancestral hunting grounds of the Cherokee, Creek, Choctaw and other Southeastern tribes. Cotton, like tobacco, quickly depleted the soil and virgin territory was needed in greater and greater amounts. By hook and crook and, when necessary, by brute force and intimidation, the land needed for the expanding cotton-growing economy was taken from the Native Americans. There were some attempts by the English Colonial Government and, after the revolution, the young American Government, to restrain the Southern farmers. Frontiers were defined—in 1763 settlement beyond the Appalachians was declared illegal, but this, like other prohibitions, was ignored from the moment it was decreed. With the new United States Government, and the newly-formed states of Alabama, Mississippi, Georgia and South Carolina, came increasing demands by white citizens for the lands still occupied by the tribes. A policy of legalized eradication of the remaining Native American communities in these States—one that denied the tribes any right to appeal the seizure of their lands—was adopted. Champions for the embattled tribes, by then known as the "Five Civilized Tribes" for their adoption of Christianity and European methods of farming, argued their case all the way to the Supreme Court and Chief Justice John Marshall. Marshall declared the policy of seizure without the right to appeal unconstitutional. President Andrew Jackson, who was determined to rid the Southeast of its native population, said, "John Marshall has rendered his decision, now let him enforce it."

Without the Executive branch of the American Government to put Marshall's decision into action, there was no stopping the encroachment of the Southern States on the last few enclaves of the Five Tribes. The final blow came in 1830, when President Jackson signed into law a bill requiring all Native people west of the Mississippi to forfeit their lands, leave their homes, and be relocated to "Indian Territory," which lay in Arkansas and Oklahoma. The Government acted quickly, first removing the Choctaw. With no State protection from bands of white settlers and no appeal of the seizure allowed, the Choctaw saw little choice but to bow to the decree and relocate. Roughly 20,000 men, women and children set out on the long journey to the new territory. Preyed upon by thieves, poorly supplied and with the Government offering little or no assistance, the Choctaw suffered enormously. More than a quarter of those who began the march died of starvation, exhaustion and disease. The Cherokee, Chickasaw, Creek and Seminole fared no better when they were removed over the next eight years. The journey to Oklahoma became known as the "Trail of Tears."

Not all of the people were willing to accept the removals. A minority of the Cherokee retreated into the most inaccessible regions of the Appalachians and defied all attempts by the Government to hunt them down. Eventually, after decades of wasted effort on the part of the United States, the remaining Cherokee were left in relative peace and granted a reservation in North Carolina in the beginning of the twentieth century. Thousands of Choctaw played a game of hide-and-seek for years in the backwoods of Mississippi and Alabama. They lived as nomads and evaded all attempts at capture while clinging to their traditions. Like the Cherokee, they also obtained lands and formed a legal reservation in central Mississippi. The Seminoles of Eastern Florida who refused to be removed took a much different approach. They formed a guerrilla army, led by a wily and determined chief, Osceola, and began a bloody conflict with federal troops that lasted seven years. Driven from the plains of Florida, they retreated further and further into the Everglades while the Government continued to waste the lives of its soldiers in a futile attempt to dislodge them. The fighting finally stopped in the 1850s and the Seminoles remained in almost complete isolation deep in the Everglades until the first half of the twentieth century. Presently, there are four reservations in Florida on or around which live the Seminole tribe.

THE PLAINS

The push west by settlers and frontiersman was relentless. As the United States grew and acquired the land through the Louisiana Purchase, the Native people of the Great Plains came into increasing contact with whites.

Following herds of buffalo that numbered in the thousands, the people of the Plains are what gave rise to many of the stereotypes found in westerns. The Cheyenne, Pawnee, Blackfeet, Sioux and Crow are some of the most familiar names and some of the largest tribes. The Plains themselves, which stretch from Texas north into southern Canada and from the Mississippi River west to the foothills of the Rocky Mountains, are a harsh environment in which to eke out an existence. The wiry grass makes the soil a tough mat of roots; extremely difficult, if not impossible to till without draft animals or metal plows. The winters are long as the wind howls south from the Arctic, bringing heavy snows and frigid temperatures with it. Before the arrival of the Europeans, with their horses and metal tools, the Plains were not heavily populated. Without the ability to raise crops, the land could not easily support villages. The larger populations, like the Pawnee, relied on the more fertile soil close to the Mississippi flood plain and areas close to the foothills of the Rockies to raise their corn and beans, venturing out onto the open prairies only to hunt the buffalo. Unlike the more eastern tribes, the diet of the Plains people was more focused on the huge herds that supported them, creating a variety of ways to prepare buffalo and elk. Once the horse was introduced to these tribes though, their way of life changed drastically. The Horse Culture of the Plains is legendary and many of the whites who witnessed it commented that never was there a people and a domesticated animal more perfectly suited for one another. In the span of two centuries, between the time the horse was introduced and the beginning of the nineteenth century, the Plains people became expert riders and breeders of the animal. The Pinto, a sturdy, small horse was originally bred by the Native Americans. Deceptively fast and strong, the Pinto was perfectly suited to hunt buffalo which, with their sharp horns and surprising maneuverability, were dangerous animals for any hunter to pursue. With the horse, tribes like the Sioux and Cheyenne became almost completely dependent on the buffalo, following them across the central plains throughout the year and living in large camps of teepees. Of all the Plains tribes however, none was more reputed for their love of the horse than the Comanche.

THE PLAINS HORSE CULTURE

Among the Comanche, both boys and girls trained from childhood with the horse, beginning as young as age four. The boys' training was more intense, as the horse had become an indispensable part of combat. They learned to ride and shoot bows and, later, rifles from horseback with deadly accuracy. Also learned was a method of using the horse as a shield. A warrior would hook his heel across the back of his mount while leaning around beneath the horse's head to fire at an enemy, all at a full gallop. The wealthier chiefs would have herds that numbered two and three hundred horses—a sign of their wealth and prestige. The animals formed dowries for brides, hauled the entire tribe and their belongings from place to place as they followed the herds across the Plains, and were a prize to be captured in raids on neighboring groups. On their flanks were painted the signs and battlefield honors of their owners. Feared warriors were recognized as much by their horses as by their faces and names, and those who had never seen or heard of them before could immediately see they were faced with a dangerous opponent by what was painted on his horse.

This dependence on the horse, and the subsequent dependence on the buffalo that arose from it, was one of the greatest weaknesses of the Plains people when their conflicts began with the whites.

Some of the tribes had already felt the pressure of the growing colonies in the east as many of the battered people, such as the remains of the Delaware and the Huron, along with stronger tribes, were forced west. The Blackfeet, Arapaho, Cheyenne, Crow, Sioux and others did not originally live exclusively on the Plains. They were tribes of the Mississippi and Missouri River Valleys but, as more and more of the eastern tribes moved west to escape the mounting difficulties with both the whites and the Iroquois, they moved out onto the open prairies.

Contact with the white man was slow and sporadic at first. The early explorers had called the Plains the "Great American Desert," and thought little or nothing of the vast, unbounded sea of windblown scrub grass. Mountain men, seeping ever west in search of furs or gold, were the first to establish trading posts, bring guns and metal utensils, and deliver smallpox and whiskey to the tribes. As it had in the East, disease ravaged the people of the Plains and some tribes, such as the Mandan, were reduced from a vital group of several thousand to less than a hundred. Whiskey was a plague in itself for the tribes. Alcoholism was a problem they had never faced before the whites appeared and they had no social mechanism to deal with the problem. When the traders saw this, some inevitably took advantage of it.

SITTING BULL, CRAZY HORSE AND THE PLAINS WARS

In the 1840s, gold was struck in California and the rush was on for settlers to stake their claims and strike it rich, or begin a new life in the California boomtowns. On the journey west, however, many saw the fertile lands of the Missouri, or those along the Oregon trail, and decided they didn't need to get all the way to the Pacific Coast to live well. These homesteaders began settling down, claiming tracts of land to farm or raise cattle and sheep. But the land they claimed was the territory of the Plains tribes— their hunting grounds and, for some, the land on which they raised their crops—and the cycle of conflict that had devastated the tribes of the East began anew.

The forty-niners traveling west were slaughtering large numbers of buffalo to stock up for the long journey, moving in large wagon trains down the trails to the Rockies and California. The U. S. Government saw the seeds of a massive conflict and, in one of its few sincere efforts to protect both the Native American tribes and the settlers moving west, called together a great council of the Northern Plains tribes. Some 10,000 people of eight tribes met with Government Agent Thomas Fitzpatrick at Fort Laramie, Wyoming, in 1851. There they signed an agreement which, in effect, guaranteed that the tribes would not attack the trains heading west, and they would abide by agreed-on territories for each tribe to end their own cycle of warfare. A sincere gesture, but one which was impossible to live up to. It meant the end of the Plains Horse Culture. No longer would the Sioux be able to raid the Crow for horses, or the Cheyenne ride the prairies following the herds of buffalo, instead they had to remain in what amounted to vast reservations and accept subsidies of supplies and equipment from the U. S. Government; they had unwittingly placed themselves under Federal control. It lasted only three years.

In 1854, a stray cow wandered into the hands of a Sioux hunter who, naturally, killed it and brought it back to camp. The rancher demanded $25 for the slaughtered animal; the Sioux said they would give him $10. Indignant, the rancher demanded the hunter be surrendered to him for the application of justice and the chief refused. A Lieutenant at Fort Laramie was called in to settle the matter. Bored and possessing a general dislike for Indians, Lieutenant John Grattan boasted he would secure the prairies for the ranchers and homesteaders with a few good men. With 30 soldiers he rode to the Sioux camp where the cow thief was said to be hiding, and demanded he be turned over. When the Sioux refused Grattan opened fire on the camp, killing the chief. Enraged, Sioux warriors swarmed over the small federal force and killed all but one. Thus began thirty years of bloody conflict between the Plains tribes and the Federal Government.

The catalog of conflict between the U. S. Government and the tribes of the Great Plains is a long series of skirmishes, some of which the tribes won, some they lost. Often set off by imaginary accusations of cow stealing or horse thievery, the standing order given to punitive raids on the offending village was "Kill them, wherever you can find them." It was usually interpreted quite literally and led to terrible massacres of men, women and children. News of the massacres, when it reached the East, was greeted by some with revulsion and outrage, considered a cold-blooded and cowardly slaughter of innocents, but even more took a charitable view of the fighting, considering the Indian to be a threat in any situation or location.

From this thirty year period of vicious bloodletting and endless revenge killing on both sides, come the names of the chiefs who are most recognized. Red Cloud, Crazy Horse and Sitting Bull have become legendary figures, sometimes villains or, more recently, tragic heroes. They were, in reality, brilliant military tacticians and charismatic leaders who clung stubbornly to their vanishing way of life. Sitting Bull was the largest-looming of them all and was considered a holy man and a prophet by his people. Together, they united the greatest force of warriors ever assembled on the Plains who, in reality, were hoping to flee what had become a war with the U. S. Government. In 1876, on the Northern Plains, in the valley of the Bighorn River, a massive encampment of Sioux and Cheyenne had gathered. They were considered the last of the renegades and General George Custer was dispatched to round them up and put an end to the "Indian troubles." With a few hundred men, Custer unwittingly launched a three-pronged attack against nearly 3,000 Plains warriors. Led by Sitting Bull, Crazy Horse and Gall, the Sioux and Cheyenne slaughtered Custer's men. It was the last and greatest victory of the Plains tribes. At the end of the summer, the encampment dissolved into smaller bands. The Army and Cavalry hunted them down one after another, finally capturing even Crazy Horse, and removing them to reservations. Sitting Bull, who fled into Canada, was finally forced to surrender in 1881. He was later shot and killed, along with his son, in a scuffle with tribal police. By the beginning of the twentieth century, the buffalo had been destroyed and there was scarcely a single tribesman still riding the Plains.

THE GREAT BASIN AND CALIFORNIA

As the battle was beginning for the tribes of the Great Plains, it was almost over before it started for the people of the Great Basin. The Basin is an area of almost 200,000 square miles that lies between the Sierra Nevadas in the west and the Wasatch Mountains in the east. In the north it is bounded by the Snake River and to the south lies the searing Mohave desert. It is, by any account, some of the most difficult terrain in America on which to make a living. High, sheer ridges separate valleys that are pounded by the summer sun and swept bare by icy winters. The annual rainfall is a scant five to seven inches. The great herds and large game that Eastern and Plains tribes relied on so heavily are nonexistent in the region making the essence of the people of the high desert's diet centered more on rabbits, ducks and wild vegetables.

Given the climate and landscape with which the tribes of the Great Basin were faced, it is not surprising that they were hunter-gatherers; nomads who roamed the vast high desert in small family groups, staying in one place only as long as they could fill their bellies. The tribes—Ute, Paiute, Bannock and Washo—were shocking to the first whites to enter the area. They seemed primitive and totally lacking in any kind of social organization other than the simple family groups that wandered aimlessly searching for a meal. This was not entirely true, though. The groups did associate themselves with larger clans, and the clans were aware of their membership in a tribe.

SURVIVAL IN THE HIGH DESERT

For them life revolved around the rhythm of the seasons. The winters, gray and bleak, were a time for simple survival. Much of what they lived off of was what had been dried and put aside to get them through these hard months—pinon nuts, seeds and smoked or sun-dried game—usually rabbit, gopher or ground squirrel . Wrapped in their rabbit-skin blankets, they ranged far in search of the stray bird or rabbit, or a last, late patch of edible roots. In springtime, the sun again appeared and with it the ground squirrels, gopher, kangaroo rats and other small game would emerge from their winter burrows. Women would wade into the icy marshes to gather cattail sprouts and the men crept across the water on rafts to flush ducks out of the reeds and into large nets of woven bark and plant fibers. As summer approached, bands would migrate to the mouths of rivers where huge schools of *cui-ui* (suckers), shiners and spring trout were beginning their spawning runs upstream. Rice grass was harvested and the seeds ground into coarse meal for bread.

Of all the seasons, fall was the time for celebration. It was when the pinon nuts ripened on the branches of scrub trees, supplying enough food for the annual gathering of the clans. They would congregate in September, near groves of pinon trees, to hold feasts and offer prayers of thanks and continued good luck with the Pinon Prayer Dance. Marriages were held, ties between families were reaffirmed and differences settled. There was no glory for them in warfare, so conflicts were settled nonviolently. For major offenses, equity was agreed upon between the parties and, in the case of casual misbehavior, the simple sting of gossip was all the punishment needed. Then, as the days faded into November, rabbit drives began. Nets were erected and the community would drive the game into them by stirring up the brush with clubs and yells. And, as the cold winds signaled the onset of winter and the pinon harvest was completed, the clans would drift away again, fragmenting into family groups until the next year.

This fragile balance was shattered almost overnight with the arrival of fortune hunters and people migrating to the promised land of California. The wagon traffic and miners disturbed and trampled the seed patches and pinon groves on which the Basin people depended for their survival. Being non-combatant, their only defense was to flee from the outsiders. With the disruption that the whites brought to the precarious balance the tribes had established over the centuries, their way of life became impossible. Reservations were set up for them on the vast tracks of land considered useless by the miners and ranchers, and there the tribes remained, their nomadic ways all but abandoned.

CALIFORNIA

In California, the situation was much the same. A much more hospitable place than the Great Basin, the tribes of California enjoyed isolation from the east, living in the shadow of the Sierra Nevadas and on the far side of the Southwestern desert. There were over 100 small tribes, including the Yokuts, Pomos, Chumash, Shasta and Miwok, and dozens of languages were spoken. It was one of the most diverse areas in North America. Blessed with the resources of the Pacific, most notably the salmon, abundant game and the acorns of the white oak, there was enough for everyone. Unlike the people of the Basin, there was a vast array of different game in the foods they commonly ate and salt was widely used to season their foods. Warfare was almost completely unknown to them. They excelled in basket weaving and, as in the case of the Pomos of Central California, created some of the finest examples of Native American basketry ever seen.

Money was minted in the form of Magnesite (a white mineral) cylinders and clamshell beads. It was used as a means of exchange in the extensive trade between different groups for seal furs, salt, obsidian (for cutting tools and arrowheads) and anything else a village thought they needed. It was also used for funerary offerings, and, in the peaceful disputes between individuals or families, to pay reparations for damages.

THE MISSION SYSTEM

The isolation of the California tribes from the east did not protect them from the arrival of the Europeans. The Spanish arrived first, cruising up the Pacific coast in their impressive galleons in the sixteenth century. At that time the Spaniards were not intent on colonizing, only finding a suitable harbor for the galleons to resupply for the journey from Mexico to the Philippines, and the Indians were left in peace. It wasn't until the eighteenth century, with the realization that the British and Russians posed a threat to their southern holdings, that they imposed the Mission system to gain control of all the people in California as they had done in Mexico. The Spaniards built a string of Catholic Missions in California. The Native people were converted to Christianity (which could be a brutal process in itself) and "civilized." The civilization of the tribes was done by stripping them of their traditional culture, and placing them in the role of farmers, herders of sheep, and workers on the ranches of the Franciscan missions. With this change came a change in diet, and an introduction to alcohol and the diseases of the Europeans that, like it had done in the east and on the Plains, nearly exterminated them. By the time California was ceded to the United States Government, those tribes who were not completely wiped out were forced onto tiny reservations save for a few, who retreated into the foothills of the Sierras. Eventually, what remained of the diversity of the California tribes, almost 133,000 people, was confined to 111 small Reservations or absorbed by the growing population of settlers.

THE PLATEAU

To the north of the California tribes lay an area around the Columbia and Frasier rivers known as the Plateau. It was home to a patchwork of different tribes and cultures. Some resembled the Northwest Canadian tribes, with pounded copper ornaments and finely carved figurines; among these groups were the Spokan, Chinook and Columbia. Others had more in common with the people of the Plains, including ties to the Shoshonean language spoken by the Cheyenne and Shoshone, their mode of dress, and forays onto the Plains after harvest-time to hunt the buffalo. These were the Nez Perce, Flathead, Umatilla and Cayuse, among others.

LIFE ON THE PLATEAU

The tribes of the Plateau did not have much in the way of political ties outside of their own villages or communities. Their leaders were more or less headmen who advised tribal councils on when feasts should be held or where their village should be moved. Trading was a thriving enterprise on the Plateau, thanks to the huge Columbia and Frasier river systems that dominated the area. The waterways allowed goods to be transported quickly and easily throughout the entire region and even to the edges of the Canadian Northwestern cultures like the Tlingit and Kwiakutl (tribes most often associated with the sub-arctic and Eskimo peoples). The real overseers of much of the east-west river trade were the Chinooks. Most of the bargaining was done in a pigeon version of the Chinook language and the tribe controlled much of the flow of wares, even exacting tolls from some river traffic.

Originally the people of the Plateau were root gatherers and salmon fishermen. There was not the same prevalence of red meat, like buffalo and venison, and corn in the foods they ate as there was among the Eastern and Plains people. The salmon fisheries of the Columbia river are the most bountiful in the world, and not surprisingly, the salmon, along with the sturgeon, was the staple of their diets. It was fished for with nets and weirs, shot with bows and speared. The meat could be smoked and saved or simply roasted and eaten immediately. Second in importance to the salmon were the wild carrots, onions and the starchy root of the wild camas (a kind of lily). The roots were used in stews or roasted and provided a food source that was abundant and could be harvested from early spring all the way up to the onset of winter. Deer hunting expeditions in the late fall and early months of winter provided not only another source of meat , but skins for bags and clothing.

The introduction of the horse to a region of fishermen and root gatherers altered the lives of some tribes drastically, most notably the Nez Perce. With new found mobility, the Nez Perce came into greater contact with the tribes of the Plains and adopted many of their ways of life. Skin teepees replaced their traditional mat-roofed lodges; their clothes took on the fringed-buckskin and intricate beadwork favored by the Sioux and Cheyenne. They became expert breeders and horsemen, maintaining large herds as did the Flatheads and other groups near the southeastern edge of the Plateau. By the first half of the nineteenth century, the people of the Columbia River were at the height of their prosperity.

CHIEF JOSEPH AND THE NEZ PERCE REBELLION

Lewis and Clark, with their Shoshone guide, Sacajewea, passed through the region in 1806. They saw the prosperity of the tribes and also the vast potential for economic development by trappers and ranchers. This was reported to the United States Government and the Oregon Trail was opened in the 1820s. Ranchers, farmers, trappers and railroad men flooded the Northwest and, as they had done elsewhere, began to covet the tribal lands. The Governor of the Washington Territory began a furious series of treaty negotiations. Bribing, threatening, and, in short, saying anything necessary to get the deal signed, Governor Isaac Stevens managed to seal 52 treaties between 1843 and 1852, gaining 157 million acres of land from the tribes of Oregon, Idaho and Washington. To add insult to injury, almost before the pen hit the paper, the treaties were violated. More land than was agreed on was taken for use by the whites; the tribes were overcrowded on reservations, often in close quarters with enemy groups; and when the people complained that their leaders were bribed or plied with alcohol to get them to sign away ancestral lands, their complaints were ignored. Rebellions began in 1855 and federal troops were brought in to crush them. The Cayuse, under chief Kamaiakian, waged a bloody war for three years until it was brought under control by the Government. Other, smaller insurrections burned briefly all across the Plateau and on the reservations until the final, and most famous conflict, put an end to the rebellions: the Nez Perce Rebellion of 1877.

Pressured into signing a treaty that forfeited the Wallowa Valley, the most prized of the Nez Perce's territory, the tribe was to be relocated to a less-than-ideal area in Idaho. They were angry and bitter about the removal and, days before they were to be marched to their reservation, a number of their horses were stolen. This proved to be the last straw and a group of young warriors retaliated, killing 18 settlers. Led by Chief Joseph, 300 warriors and 500 women and children led the U. S. Army on a 1,600-mile chase through the rugged hills of the Plateau. The chase was marked with skirmishes and the brilliant strategy of Chief Joseph, who managed to outmaneuver General Oliver O. Howard for weeks. Heading for Canada, hoping to join Sitting Bull and the remains of his band of Sioux who had escaped across the border after Little

Bighorn, the Army finally caught up to Joseph and his warriors at Snake Creek, thirty miles from the border. With Chiefs Looking Glass and White Bird, 300 of Joseph's Nez Perce made a run for Canada while Chief Joseph, outnumbered, stayed behind with remainder of his people, preparing to surrender. His surrender was delivered in a memorable speech to General Howard, and recorded by an interpreter: "Hear me my Chiefs. I am tired. My heart is sick and sad. From where the sun now stands, I will fight no more forever." And, with Chief Joseph's words, the last of the rebellions in the Northwest ended.

THE SOUTHWEST

Of all the Native American people, none withstood the waves of settlers longer than those of the Southwest. Arizona, New Mexico and West Texas is a majestic landscape of flat-topped mesas, deep ravines and canyons, wild mountains and fierce, sun-hardened deserts. It can rise well over 100 degrees in the afternoon and plummet to near-freezing at night. And, not surprisingly, it was not an area heavily settled by whites until late in the nineteenth century; even today the population remains relatively sparse—wide-open spaces punctuated by small towns and only a few large cities.

THE PUEBLOS

Long before the coming of the Spanish or American settlers, the climate was not quite so arid as it is today and four groups—the Mogollon, Anasazi, Hohokan and Patayan—built their civilizations there. Except for what has been found at archeological sites such as Mesa Verde and Kayenta, little is known about these people. What these sites reveal is a sophisticated and thriving culture. They are cities of cliff dwellings that supported upwards of 1,000 people in their heyday. Masters at making the desert bloom through irrigation farming, the four ancient tribes of the Southwest reached their pinnacle around 700 A. D., much like the Maya of Southern Mexico. They did not destroy themselves through internecine warfare, as is now believed the Maya did, but were forced to abandon their cities slowly during 250 years of drought beginning sometime around 1200 or 1300 A. D. Even with their knowledge of irrigation farming, which had served them so well for centuries, the region became too dry to support such large communities. The people never really disappeared though, they simply adapted to the new conditions of the desert. They became what are now called the Pueblos, a name given collectively to the various groups that inhabit adobe and mud brick complexes reminiscent of those at Mesa Verde. They are people like the Yavapais and Walapais, who descended from the Patayan, the Hopi and Zuni, who descended from the Anasazi, and the Pima and Papago, descendants of the Hohokan. Their villages, called Pueblos, are along the rivers that flow through the Southwest: the Rio Grande and Colorado.

Primarily farmers, the Pueblo people raised corn, beans, tobacco, squash and melons, and relied (much like the people of the Great Basin) less on game than the tribes in other regions of the continent. In the desert, sufficient water is a constant problem and they developed strategies to cope with this. Several pueblos would cooperate in digging irrigation ditches, some stretching for miles, to bring water to the small plots planted on the flatlands below the villages. The type of corn grown, a short, hardy and quick to mature variety, was bred specifically to withstand the rigors of the desert climate. It was planted deep—12 to 16 inches in the ground—where the young plants could sprout in the damp, cooler soil and anchor themselves firmly to withstand the frequent windstorms and occasional gully-washing rains.

The Pueblos' villages, built mainly on the defensible high ground of the mesas, were all organized in the same general manner. One of the best examples is the Hopi pueblo of Oraibi, which has been continuously populated for the last 1000 years. Multi-roomed buildings of adobe and mud brick are organized around central *kivas*—large communal buildings used as a gathering place for the men and for ceremonies. They are stone-walled and often sunk deep in the ground. It symbolizes the connection of the world above to the world below, from which come the spirits that inhabit all things animate and inanimate. These spirits each have a specific role to play in maintaining the equilibrium of the cosmos. The Hopi saw their role as living with good hearts and observing their rituals. One misunderstood (but often portrayed in films or pulp novels) rite is the Snake Ceremonial. The rite was performed by the Snake and Antelope religious societies and lasted for nine days. After several days of prayer, the men went into the desert and gathered snakes, poisonous and non-, and brought them to the kiva. The serpents, believed to have the ability to tell whether a man has a good and fearless heart, were given ritual baths and dried with sand, then placed around the necks of the dancers. At sunset on the ninth day the snakes were carried in the mouths of the men as they danced around the plaza, then taken and released into the desert to spread word of the Hopis' prayers to all other creatures and bring much-needed rain.

THE NAVAJO AND APACHE

In the 1400s, migrant groups filtered into the Southwest. They were the Apacheans who, over time subdivided into two related but distinct people: the Navajo and the Apache. Nomadic or semi-nomadic, these two groups were vastly different from the people of the Pueblos. They were hunter-gatherers who relied, much like the people of the Great Basin, on the rhythm of the seasons. They traveled in bands usually no larger than a few extended families and did not build the lasting types of structures that people such as the Hopi and Yavapai did. One outstanding feature of their lifestyle that was quickly adopted after moving into the region was raiding. Through the eyes of Hollywood, they are viewed as wild marauders, cutting bloody paths through the desert, swooping down on settlers and Pueblo villages alike. They did have a reputation as fierce raiders, and were feared and respected for this by the sedentary people of the region, but they were not the indiscriminate killers that many believe them to be. Raiding was not warfare for them, it was simply part of how they made their living. Killing in raids brought no special status or glory and they did not collect scalp locks or trophies. The history of the Apache, Navajo and other people of the Southwest (including the Europeans) is one of a series of fluctuating alliances formed on the basis of economic advantage. There was no conquest or subjugation, only a view to what was best for the needs of a family or band at any given time.

Both groups adopted agriculture from the Pueblos and used it in a limited way to supplement their existence. They hunted the rabbit, antelope and other game in the region, but did not rely so heavily on venison like the Southeastern tribes or large herds like the Plains people, and traditional foods from the region reflect this. The Navajo came to rely more heavily on farming than the Apache did and, after the Spanish began to settle in the area during the seventeenth century, adopted herding as well, eventually gaining a reputation for their skill with livestock. The Apache, who lived mainly in protected highlands and canyons, did not become herders until they were forced onto reservations late in the nineteenth century but continued to use raiding as the basis of their economy.

THE SPANISH AND THE PUEBLO RESISTANCE

When the Europeans arrived in the region, they brought change to the Pueblos and Navajo, but had a relatively small impact on the Apache. The Spaniards arrived first, looking for gold and souls to save. Their methods were brutal, as they were elsewhere, and involved consistent terrorization of those who would not accept Christianity. Individuals were beaten, hung, burned at the stake and garroted for clinging to their old ceremonies and beliefs and many were forced to labor for the Conquistadors and Missions. Some of the Pueblos formally adopted Christianity, hoping to alleviate some of the brutality but, just as the kiva was the center of their villages, their ancient religion was the center of their lives and it continued on in spite of the Missions' belief that they were stamping it out.

Rebellions, scattered and desperate, were crushed by the invaders as soon as they began and the bitter Pueblos soon realized that only a united effort could be successful. In 1680, led by a medicine man from one of the Rio Grande Pueblos, an orchestrated attack using the combined strength of the villages killed 400 Spanish soldiers and priests and left their churches and ranch houses in ashes. The Indian army then mounted a fierce and relentless attack on Santa Fe, driving the Spanish out and reducing the town to ruins. Twelve years later, the missionaries returned, trying to save the souls of the Pueblo people. They were ordered to leave, but refused and converted several people of one village. When the Hopi at Oraibi heard of this, word spread quickly and the surrounding villages descended on the Spaniards, killing every man, woman and child, and setting ablaze everything that would burn. The slaughter taught the Spanish a painful lesson and they left the Pueblos to live their quiet lives as farmers and to practice their ancient religion.

The people of the Southwest—Spaniards, Apaches, Navajo and Pueblos—settled into a tenuous existence resembling what the region had experienced previous to the appearance of the Europeans—the Apaches and Navajo raided, and the sedentary people, now the Pueblos and Spaniards, defended themselves and formed temporary alliances that were mutually beneficial with groups of Apaches or Navajos. Guns and horses were introduced (the Apaches became especially enamored of the horse, like the Cheyenne and Comanche, and were outstanding riders), and herding was adopted by the Navajo. But, with the independence of Mexico, and the westward push of the American frontier in the nineteenth century, things began to change drastically. The Mexican and American Governments looked to the Southwest and saw the raiding Apache and Navajo as something that needed to be brought under control, along with many of the staunchly defiant Pueblos.

The Pueblos, which had become heavily fortified villages over centuries of fending off raids and fighting the Spanish, were no easy target for the Mexican Army and the settlers and miners who were greedy for their lands. A slow, relentless period of skirmishes and sieges reduced the number of Pueblos from 90 to 30 over the course of the first half of the nineteenth century, with the last of the most fiercely defiant people, the Yaquis, finally being overrun in the mid-1800s. Many of the villages, due to their location or their deliberate low profile in dealing with the Mexican Government, were left alone and remain intact today.

THE "LONG WALK"

The Navajo and Apache suffered a much different fate than the Pueblos. Their raiding was viewed as a threat—lawlessness at a time when order was desperately trying to establish itself in the Southwest. The Mexican and American Governments both, responding to the complaints of white ranchers, miners and California-bound settlers, embarked on a campaign to rid the area of the nomads. The plan of the U. S. Government was to force a change in the primary way of life followed by the two peoples. They decided to pin them down on Reservations, supply them with livestock and transform the tribes into peaceful ranchers. The plan was given to Kit Carson, a famed hunter and "Indian Fighter" who began herding bands of Apaches to Fort Sumner and the Reservation established at Redondo, on the Pecos River. The Navajo had no desire to be torn from their way of life and planted on a 40-square-mile reservation, and the army was forced to adopt harsh measures to implement their plan. Kit Carson began a scorched-earth policy, killing the flocks, burning the crops, destroying the earthen dwellings (*hogans*), corrals and storehouses of the Navajo, and shooting those Indians who would not surrender. Starving and disheartened, thousands of Navajo finally began coming out of hiding in the hills, surrendering to promises of food, clothing and a new life on the Reservation. What they found, however, was little food, no clothing and a 300 mile march to Redondo that became known as "The Long Walk" and killed many of the cold and starving people. Redondo itself was a desolate stretch of land where crops wouldn't grow, there was no wood for fires or shelters and the Navajo were crowded in with their enemies, the Apache. Finally, after several years of this misery, a new Reservation—3.5 million acres—was granted to the Navajo within the borders of their traditional territory. They began there with nothing, and soon the Railroad began taking lands and settlers crept closer and closer to the borders of the Reservation, bringing alcohol and disease with them. The Navajo managed to survive somehow and, after years of misery and hardship, rebuild at least some of what had been taken from them.

THE APACHE WARS

The Apaches were the last, and most ruthlessly pursued of the Southwestern Indians. Expert guerrilla fighters, mobile and able to disappear almost without a trace into the wild desert highlands, they were better able to resist the tireless efforts of the American Government to round them up and place them on Reservations. The Mexican Government, subject to constant raids in Sonora and Chihuahua, did not even entertain the notion of Reservations. They were mired in a campaign to destroy the Apache, and their methods, in addition to simple slaughter, included enslaving them and sending them to the Yucatan and forcing captured women and girls into prostitution. The raids of the Apache into Northern Mexico became tempered with bitter hatred and their attacks were no longer just for food and livestock but acts of revenge. Meanwhile, in Arizona and New Mexico, the settlers were fearful of the possibility of Apache raids, their fear exacerbated by exaggerated tales of bloody attacks on peaceful white farmers. They formed volunteer militias to protect themselves and these trigger-happy bands of ranchers and homesteaders hounded the Apaches, drawing increased retaliation from them. Finally, the United States Government, which had failed to confine the Apache to Reservations, changed tactics. They began a war of extermination. What followed were several years of bloody skirmishes as the Army hunted the Apache, and the Apache outmaneuvered them and engaged in hit-and-run fighting. Cochise, Red Sleeves and Geronimo became legendary in their years of defiance against the United States Army. Eventually, after years of this eye-for-an-eye fighting, almost all of the Apaches who had not been killed had been relocated to Reservations in the Southwest and Oklahoma. Geronimo, with his band of Chiricahua Apaches, was the last resistance fighter in the region, and he was finally forced to surrender in 1886, ending the Apache Wars and the armed resistance of the Native American tribes across the United States.

THE TWENTIETH CENTURY

After Geronimo's surrender, interest in the Native American people quickly faded and knowledge of them became that of romanticized tales or demonic portrayals. By the early part of the twentieth century, the general Anglo-American public knew little of what occurred with the many tribes on the Reservations or living among them. Their history continued, however.

Initially, conditions on many of the Reservations were deplorable. They were underfunded and people who were once self-sufficient and free were left with little to do. Forced assimilation programs were started in some places: schooled with mottoes like, "Kill the Indian and save the man." Enrollment in schools and colleges was often low, the infant mortality rate was astronomically high, and railroads, loggers and other industries near tribal lands continued to whittle away at what was left to the Native Americans. This is not to say that the half-million or so Indians across the country were utterly destitute. Many of the Apaches prospered as ranchers in the Southwest. The Cherokee, Choctaw and others who had been relocated to Oklahoma had rebuilt their lives to a large extent, as did the Navajo. The Hopi and Pima, along with the other remaining Pueblos, held on to their old ways and adapted to the increasing white settlement in the region.

World War II was the beginning of a new era for many. It took thousands to urban areas to work in the factories and to serve in the Army. For a large number of them, it was their first real contact with the urban culture that had grown up around them. A new political consciousness developed on the Reservations. The National Committee of American Indians was formed to protect their rights and sue the Government and those who attempted to take tribal lands. A serious setback for many in the 1950s was the policy of Termination. The Federal Government, bowing to pressure by special interests and some public outcry against the continued subsidization of the Reservations and aid to Native American people, tried to do away with some of the Reservations. They divided the land into plots, making it individually owned property. The outcome was the loss of large amounts of land by some tribes, and hundreds were completely dispossessed. Thankfully, this policy was quickly abandoned.

The 1960s, under the Kennedy and Johnson administrations, saw the first increase in tribal lands, and in 1961, the National Indian Youth Council was formed to fight Government policies aimed at control and work toward programs that offered assistance that would help them develop their own programs and policies. Education in Reservation schools and universities rose dramatically in the 1970s (college enrollment on Reservations went from 2,000 to 35,000) and with it political activism increased, fighting assimilation and integration.

The battles continue over self determination for the tribes, over logging rights and development of natural resources such as oil and coal on tribal lands, and sporadic attempts to undermine some of the legal protection that the Indians and their advocates have secured (like the American Indian Religious Freedom Act) and, perhaps most difficult of all, stereotypes and racial prejudice. Over the last 25 years what has been called a "Renaissance" of Native American culture has resulted in new translations of the old tales and myths originally recorded in the nineteenth century, new efforts by individual tribes to retain their languages and renewals by some of religious practices that had begun to fade. Authors like Linda Hogan, Simon Ortiz and Joy Harjo are now widely read and respected, offering a perspective rooted in their heritage but filled with contemporary vitality. Literature, art and programs in schools and universities continue to try to dispel the myths perpetuated since the first, fateful contact with the people of the Americas was made three centuries ago. What is coming to light in this expanding view of the history, traditions, and ways of life of the many tribes is not a new interest in something preserved from bygone days. It is the resurgence of vital, rich and complex cultures that have persevered and adapted to every obstacle, and continue to move into the future.

The 300-plus recipes that follow are not reconstructed from old anthropological studies or reports of early explorers. A mixture of the old and the new, they are part of the continuing traditions and growing cultures that form the basis of everyday life for hundreds of thousands of people living in North America today.

✳ CHAPTER ONE ✳
LARGE GAME

DEER

Deer, as well as other big game animals, will taste better when killed properly with a good, clean, quick shot. A poorly placed shot will cause the animal to suffer pain and stress. This causes a chemical reaction in the meat, giving it a stronger, gamier taste. Venison has a delicious, distinctive flavor and is very healthy, containing one third the calories of an equivalent serving of beef.

The difference in taste between deer also depends heavily on their diet. A swamp buck will have a much stronger taste than a corn-fed deer. If necessary, we recommend marinating to sweeten the taste of any game meat. See the recipes that follow, as well as the sauces and marinades in Chapter 7.

WHITETAIL DEER

The whitetail deer is the most plentiful big game animal found in North America, with a population numbering in the millions. The typical whitetail stands 36 to 40 inches high at the shoulder. The average weight is 150 pounds, with record-breakers tipping the scales at 400 pounds plus.

The whitetail is named for its characteristic *flag*, the white underside of its tail, which shows when the tail is raised in flight. Whitetails range from the southern edge of the coniferous forest in Canada all the way south into Mexico. They are rarely found in the arid areas of the American West.

MULE DEER/BLACKTAIL DEER

Mullies and blacktails lack the distinctive swept-forward rack of the whitetail. The mule deer is somewhat heavier than the whitetail and stands taller—40–42 inches at the shoulder. *Mullies* named for their mule-like ears, range from the Pacific coast east to Texas and from Minnesota north to Alaska and south into Mexico.

The blacktail is a smaller cousin of the mule deer, being smaller and lighter even than the typical whitetail. Blacktails are found primarily in a narrow region running along the Pacific coast from Alaska to central California.

VENISON RIBS AND SAUCE

Brine made from 1 part
 vinegar to 3 parts water
5 lbs. venison ribs
2 bay leaves

2 tbsp. salt
1 onion, sliced
melted margarine

RIB SAUCE:

1 1/2 cups water
1 cup chili sauce
1/4 cup steak sauce

2 tbsp. lemon juice
1/2 tsp. chili powder
1/2 tsp. salt

Make enough brine from vinegar and water to cover ribs. Add bay leaves, salt and onions. Marinate for 48 hours in refrigerator. Drain and pat dry. Place ribs in a shallow pan and brush ribs with melted margarine. Roast for 30 minutes at 450°F. Baste once again with margarine and reduce heat to 350°F. In saucepan combine sauce ingredients; bring to a boil over medium heat. Pour rib sauce over the ribs and bake for 1 1/2 to 2 hours, basting often.

"...And the Eagle called Hoey', the Deer, and told him, 'Hoey, you are going to be good meat for the new people. They are going to kill you but, as soon as they do, you will leave your meat for them and go away and live again. You will not die."

—Yokut tale

VENISON SHEPHERD'S PIE

1/4 cup shortening
1 onion, chopped
1 1/2 lbs. ground venison
1 cup beef gravy
1 cup cooked carrots

1 cup peas
3 cups mashed potatoes
margarine
paprika

Melt shortening in a skillet. Add onions and cook until transparent. Add ground venison and fry until well browned. Drain. Pour venison and onion mixture into a 2-quart casserole. Mix in gravy. Add carrots and peas in alternate layers, then cover mixture with mashed potatoes. Dot with margarine, and sprinkle with paprika.

Bake at 400°F for 25 to 30 minutes.

FROZEN DEER LIVER FRY

1 lb. fresh deer liver
1/4 cup flour
1 tsp. basil

1/2 tsp. salt
1/4 tsp. pepper

Soak liver for two hours in salt water. Drain and pat dry. Freeze whole liver. Slice liver while frozen into thin slices. Mix flour in the seasonings. Dredge each liver slice in seasoned flour. Pan-fry in oil over medium heat until tender.

MEATBALL STEW

1 egg
1 lb. ground venison
1/2 tsp. salt
pinch of garlic powder
pinch of basil
pinch of oregano
pinch of pepper
1 tbsp. vegetable oil

2 tbsp. flour
1 (28 oz.) can tomatoes
1 (19 oz.) can whole potatoes,
   drained
2 cups frozen carrots
1 tsp. basil
1/2 tsp. oregano
salt and pepper to taste

Beat egg in large bowl, mix in ground venison, salt and pinch of each seasoning. Mix thoroughly and shape venison mixture into 2-inch balls. Heat oil in a deep skillet and add meatballs. Cook until well browned and then remove from skillet. Pat excess grease from meatballs and drain skillet. Return meat to pot and sprinkle lightly with flour. Stir in tomatoes, vegetables, oregano, and salt and pepper to taste. Reduce heat and simmer for 15 minutes.

VENISON CURRY

1 lb. venison shoulder, cut into 1
   inch cubes
Oil
3 tbsp. fat
2 cloves garlic, minced

2 medium-sized onions, sliced
1 tbsp. curry powder
1 cup tomatoes (canned)
1/2 cup raisins
Salt

Sear venison in hot oil. Remove from heat and set aside. In a heavy skillet heat the 3 tablespoons of fat. When hot, add garlic and onions. Cook until lightly browned. Stir in curry powder. Add the tomatoes and raisins and simmer for 10 minutes. Add venison cubes to tomato mixture. Season with salt and simmer for 1 1/2 hours. Add water when necessary to maintain liquid level.

VENISON BALLS

2 lbs. ground venison
2 eggs, slightly beaten
2 cups cooked rice
1/4 cup water
2 tbsp. hickory-flavored
   barbecue sauce

1 oz. soy sauce
1/2 tsp. chili pepper
1 tsp. salt
1/2 tsp. pepper
Prepared spaghetti sauce

Mix together all ingredients except spaghetti sauce, and shape into balls. Lay balls in the bottom of a roasting pan and cover with spaghetti sauce. Bake at 325°F.

SCALLOPED VENISON AND POTATO DINNER

4 potatoes, peeled and sliced
Salt and pepper
2 onions, peeled and sliced
1 lb. ground venison
2 cups spaghetti sauce
1 tbsp. brown sugar
1/4 cup grated cheese
1/4 cup crushed cornflakes

Arrange a layer of potatoes sliced in the bottom of a greased 8" baking dish. Sprinkle with salt and pepper, then add a layer of onions. Break up meat and spread over onions. Add remaining potatoes, then onions. Cover with spaghetti sauce. Sprinkle brown sugar over top. Cover and bake at 350°F for 30 minutes. Uncover and sprinkle with cheese, and cornflakes. Continue to bake for an additional 30 minutes.

VENISON MEAT BALLS IN PEPPER SAUCE

1 lb. ground venison
1/2 lb. minced pork
2 eggs, well beaten
1/2 cup bread crumbs
1/4 cup milk
1 1/2 tsp. salt
1/4 tsp. savory
Flour
3 tbsp. salad oil
1 onion, sliced
2 cloves garlic minced
1 green pepper, sliced
1 can mixed vegetables, undrained
1 tsp. beef extract
1 cup water
1 bay leaf
1 tsp. chili powder
2 tsp. chili peppers

Mix first seven ingredients together and shape into balls about 1 inch in diameter. Roll in flour. Heat salad oil in a skillet; pan-fry meatballs until brown, then transfer to a deep saucepan. Reheat oil in skillet and add onion, garlic and green peppers. Cook till onion is transparent; then add remaining ingredients and simmer for 10 minutes. Thicken slightly if desired. Pour hot sauce over the meatballs and simmer for 15 minutes.

PICKLED VENISON HEART

1 venison heart
1 tsp. salt
2 small bay leaves

1 onion, sliced
liquid to cover (3 parts water/1
   part vinegar)

Place heart in a large saucepan and add enough water to cover. Add salt and bay leaves. Bring to a boil, then reduce heat to simmer. Cover and cook until meat is tender. Drain, cool and slice heart thinly. Place slices in a bowl along with onion and water-vinegar mixture (enough to cover meat pieces). Salt and pepper to taste. Refrigerate for 3 hours. Remove meat from water-vinegar solution, pat dry and use in sandwiches as you would roast beef.

BAKED VENISON HEART
WITH ONIONS

1 venison heart
2 tbsp. flour

2 1/2 cups stewed tomatoes
6 medium onions

STUFFING:

1 cup bread crumbs
1 1/2 tsp. salt
1/2 tsp. sage

1/4 tsp. pepper
3 tbsp. margarine
2 tbsp. bacon fat

Wash venison heart and remove large veins and arteries. Fill cavity left by removing veins with bread stuffing. Sew heart to hold stuffing in. Melt bacon fat in a frying pan and brown heart on all sides after rolling in flour. Place heart in a roasting pan and pour stewed tomatoes over it and group onions around. Cover and bake at 275°F for 3 hours.

COOKED VENISON TONGUE

1 fresh venison tongue
1 onion, sliced
1 bay leaf

1 tsp. salt
Pepper

Cover tongue with cold water in a heavy pot and add remaining ingredients. Simmer until tongue is tender. Remove tongue from pot and cool slightly. Remove tissue and skin. Slice tongue and serve.

Along the edge of the village, the Deer runs swiftly and escapes his pursuers
Although he runs along the edge in his flight,
The arrows of his pursuers flying about him in forked lines,
He escapes all dangers.
The little ones shall make the Deer a symbol of courage.
—Osage Rite of Vigil

BOILED VENISON TONGUE

1 venison tongue
1 tbsp. mixed pickling spice
1/2 tsp. salt per pound of
  venison

Juice of 1 lemon
2 bay leaves
1/4 cup dry celery leaves

Scrub tongue thoroughly and place in a pot and cover with boiling water. Add remaining ingredients. Bring to a boil and cook for another 2 hours. Remove skins and root ends. Serve with horseradish sauce.

HORSERADISH SAUCE:

4 tbsp. butter, melted
2 tbsp. flour
1 cup milk

6 tbsp. prepared horseradish
1/4 tsp. salt

In a saucepan, melt butter. Blend in flour until smooth. Then, gradually, stir in milk. Last, stir in horseradish and salt and cook over medium heat until thickened. Add salt and pepper to taste.

WILD GAME PIE

CRUST:

2 cups flour
2 tbsp. baking powder
1 tsp. salt

2 tbsp. butter or margarine
1 egg
Milk

Mix together flour, baking powder, and salt. Cut in butter. Beat egg with a little milk and add to dry ingredients. Add enough extra milk to make the crust like a pie dough. Divide in half and set aside.

FILLING

5 lbs. moose or venison, cubed
Salt and pepper

2 onions, chopped
1 tsp. cinnamon

In a small roasting pan spread out half the cubed meat. Salt and pepper meat. Sprinkle 1 chopped onion and 1/2 tsp. cinnamon over meat. Roll out half the dough and cover the meat mixture. On top of this first piece of pastry spread the remaining meat cubes, salt and pepper. Sprinkle remaining onion and cinnamon on top. Cover with remaining rolled-out pastry. Bake at 250°F for 5 to 6 hours.

SWEET AND SOUR POT ROAST

2 tbsp. cooking oil
4 lbs. chuck roast (venison,
    moose)
1 cup chopped onion
1 tsp. salt
1/4 tsp. pepper

1/2 tsp. dried thyme
1/3 cup cider vinegar
1/2 cup broth
1/3 cup liquid honey
1 tbsp. cornstarch
1/4 cup water

Heat oil in heavy saucepan. Add meat and brown on all sides. Remove meat. Add onion to hot oil, stirring constantly for 3 minutes. Return meat to saucepan and sprinkle with salt, pepper and thyme. Add vinegar and broth; then cover, and simmer for 2 hours. Add honey and continue simmering until tender (approx. 1 hour more). Remove meat to hot platter. Bring liquid in saucepan to a full boil. Mix cornstarch and water together, then add to liquid gradually. Stir until thickened and clear. Turn down and simmer for 3 minutes. Serve over meat slices.

FIVE-HOUR STEW

1 1/2 lb. venison
6 carrots, sliced
4 medium-sized potatoes, sliced
1 cup celery, chopped
1 onion, sliced
1 can tomatoes

1 can beef broth
1 tbsp. sugar
5 tbsp. Minute tapioca
2 tsp. salt
V8 brand vegetable juice
    cocktail

Put all ingredients except vegetable juice cocktail into a large pot. Mix. Cover with V8 juice plus 2 inches. Cover; simmer for 5 hours at 350°F. Stir occasionally.

MILLIE'S VENISON MEATBALLS

2 lbs. ground venison
2 cups soda crackers, crumbled
1 tsp. salt
1 tsp. pepper
2 eggs

6 large onions, sliced
4 cans (10 oz. each) tomato
    soup
1 cup water

Combine ground meat, soda crackers, salt, pepper and eggs. Mix thoroughly. Form into medium-sized meatballs. Brown well in a large, heavy pot. Melt cooking fat in a large skillet. Saute onions until softened and slightly browned. Combine onions and tomato soup in the large pot with meatballs. Pour in the water and mix thoroughly. Cover and simmer for 1 1/2 to 2 hours, stirring occasionally. Serve with whipped potatoes or just with Mom's Salad.

CURRIED VENISON AND VEGETABLES

1 tbsp. vegetable oil
1 lb. ground venison
3 cups shredded cabbage
2 carrots, peeled and sliced
2 stalks celery, sliced
1 green pepper, cored and
    thinly sliced

1 onion, peeled and chopped
1 cup broth
1 1/2 to 2 tsp. curry powder
1 1/2 tsp. salt
1 tsp. pepper
1 1/2 cups dried macaroni
2 tbsp. chopped parsley

Heat oil in a cooking pot and brown the ground venison. Drain excess fat. Add cabbage, carrots, celery, green pepper and onion. Stir in broth and seasonings. Bring to a boil, then reduce heat and simmer until vegetables are tender. Meanwhile, prepare macaroni as directed on the package. Drain and add macaroni to the broth and vegetable mixture. Garnish with parsley and serve.

MEATY TOMATO DUMPLINGS

1 small onion, chopped
1 tbsp. salad oil
1/2 lb. ground venison
1/4 tsp. garlic powder
1/4 tsp. sage

1 tsp. salt
3/4 cup sifted pastry flour
1 tsp. baking powder
1 egg (well beaten)
2 tbsp. milk

Saute onion in oil until softened. Add meat and seasonings. Stir-fry gently until meat is cooked. Remove from heat and cool slightly.

In a bowl, sift flour and baking powder together. Add egg and milk and mix thoroughly; then mix in meat mixture.

Bring soup, water and tomato juice to a boil and add heaping spoonfuls of the dumpling mixture. Cover and steam-cook for 15 minutes. Serves 4 people.

Deer, you stand close by the tree,
You sweeten your mouth with acorns,
Now you are standing near,
You have come where your food rests on the ground.

—Cherokee hunting song

VENISON BROILED BURGERS

2/3 cup soft bread crumbs
1/4 cup minced onion
pepper
1/4 tsp. sage

1 tbsp. catsup or tomato juice
1 tbsp. milk
1 lb. ground venison meat
4 slices bacon

Mix bread crumbs, onion, horseradish, salt, pepper, sage, catsup and milk with ground meat. Shape into 4 patties. Wrap a piece of bacon around each patty and secure with toothpick. Broil each side until done, about 12 to 16 minutes.

HEAVENLY HASH

2 slices bacon
1 large onion
2 stalks celery
1 1/2 lbs. venison burger
3 cups cooked macaroni

1 can tomato soup
1 can mushroom soup
  (undiluted)
1/2 cup grated cheese

Cook bacon crisp and set aside: reserve drippings. Dice onion and celery. Brown meat, onion and celery in bacon drippings. Add macaroni to meat mixture. Add remaining ingredients including crumbled bacon. Place in casserole dish. Bake at 350°F for 45 minutes.

EASY VENISON

Liver Skillet
1 lb venison liver
1/4 cup all-purpose flour
1/4 cup butter
1 medium onion, sliced thinly
1 can (19 oz.) tomatoes
1 tsp. sugar

1 tsp. salt
1 tsp. Worcestershire sauce
1/4 tsp. basil or curry
dash of pepper
1 1/2 cups shredded cheddar
  cheese

Cut liver into 1/2-inch strips and coat lightly with flour. Melt butter in frying pan; add liver and brown quickly on both sides. Add onion and fry gently until almost tender. Stir in tomatoes, sugar, salt, Worcestershire sauce, basil and pepper.

Cover and simmer gently for approximately 15 minutes. Add cheese and stir until melted. If served in a casserole, garnish with additional cheese and broil until golden. Serve alone or over boiled rice.

FRIED VENISON LIVER

1 1/2 lbs venison liver, sliced
3 tbsp. lemon juice
1/2 cup flour
1 tsp. basil
1/2 tsp. salt
1/4 tsp. pepper

2 eggs, beaten
1/2 cup cream
1 onion, grated
1 tsp. garlic powder
2 cups dried bread crumbs
1/2 cup bacon fat

Sprinkle liver with lemon juice. Combine flour, basil, salt and pepper. Dredge liver slices completely. Mix together eggs, cream, onion, and garlic powder. Dip the liver into this mixture and then dip into bread crumbs. Fry quickly on both sides in hot bacon fat.

VENISON MEATBALLS AND MUSHROOMS

1 lb ground venison
1 egg beaten
3/4 cup bread or cracker crumbs
1/2 tsp. salt
1 tsp. celery salt

1/4 tsp. pepper
3/4 tsp. nutmeg
1 can mushrooms
1 cup water
1 pkg. mushroom gravy mix

In a bowl, combine meat, egg, crumbs, salts, pepper and nutmeg. Mix well and then shape into balls. In a skillet brown meatballs over medium heat. Drain.

Place meatballs in a casserole dish and pour in mushrooms and liquid. Add the water and the gravy mix. Cover and bake at 350°F for 1/2 hour.

PORCUPINES

1 lb. venison burger
1/2 cup uncooked rice
1/2 cup water
1/3 cup onion, chopped
1 tsp. salt
1/2 tsp. celery salt

1/8 tsp. garlic powder
1/8 tsp. pepper
1 can (15 oz) tomato sauce
1 cup water
2 tsp. Worcestershire sauce

In a bowl, mix burger, rice, water, onion, salt, celery salt, garlic powder and pepper together. Form into balls. Cook meatballs in a skillet until brown, and then drain off the grease. Mix remaining ingredients and pour over meatballs. Heat to boiling and then reduce heat. Cover and simmer for 45 minutes (add more water during cooking if necessary).

MEATLOAF

1 1/2 lbs. ground venison
1 cup quick-cooking rolled oats
2 eggs, beaten
1 cup milk
1/4 cup onion, chopped

1 tsp. prepared mustard
2 tsp. salt
1/4 tsp. pepper
1 can (10 oz.) cream of
  mushroom soup, undiluted

Mix together all ingredients, except 1/2 can of the cream of mushroom soup, and press into loaf pan. Spread the remaining soup on top of the meat loaf. Bake at 375°F for 1 hour.

GLAZED VENISON LOAF

2 lbs. ground venison
2 eggs
1 cup sour cream
1/4 cup grated onion
1 cup dry bread crumbs
1 tbsp. parsley

2 tbsp. Worcestershire sauce
1/2 tsp. salt
1/4 tsp. pepper
1/2 cup tomato sauce
1 1/2 tsp. corn syrup
1 tbsp. Worcestershire sauce

Mix together first 7 ingredients, and season with salt and pepper. Shape into a greased loaf pan and place in a 350°F oven for 45 to 50 minutes. When pan is cool, turn meat out onto a baking sheet. Mix together tomato sauce, corn syrup and the 1 tablespoon Worcestershire sauce. Pour mixture over meat and bake for an additional 15 minutes.

VENISON-BURGER CASSEROLE

1 onion, chopped
1/2 cup chopped green pepper
1/4 cup margarine
1 lb. minced venison

1 lb. macaroni
1 can (10 oz.) tomato soup,
  diluted with water
1 lb. milk cheese, sliced thin

Saute onions and green pepper in 1 tablespoon of the margarine. Add venison; brown with onion and pepper. Drain. Prepare macaroni according to package directions. Put macaroni in a large casserole; add hamburger, onion and pepper, stir in the tomato soup and cheese. Dot with remaining margarine. Bake for 20 minutes at 350°F.

SHIPWRECK DINNER

4 large potatoes, peeled and
    sliced thick
1 large onion, thinly sliced
1 lb. minced venison
1/4 cup raw rice

1 cup chopped celery
1 can 10 oz. tomato soup,
    diluted
Margarine

In a greased casserole, put a layer of potatoes, a layer of onion and a layer of ground venison. Sprinkle rice over the meat. Distribute celery over the top and pour in the prepared tomato soup. Dot with margarine. Cover and bake at 325°F for 2 hours.

CHILI CON CARNE

1 lb. venison burger
1 large onion, chopped
1 to 2 stalks celery, chopped
1 can tomatoes
1 can kidney beans

1 can tomato soup or paste
1 to 2 tbsp. chili powder
Garlic salt
Salt and pepper

Brown burger in skillet and add onion and celery. In a large pot combine burger mixture and remaining ingredients and simmer 15 minutes.

CHILARONI

1 lb. venison burger
1 onion, chopped
1 can (28 oz.) tomatoes
8 oz. tomato sauce

2 tbsp. chili powder
1 (10 oz. can) kidney beans
3 cups cooked macaroni

Place burger and onions in a skillet and cook until meat is lightly browned. Drain. Add remaining ingredients to the skillet. Simmer for 25 to 30 minutes.

I know not if the voice of man can reach the sky;
I know not if the mighty one will hear my prayers;
I know not if the gifts I ask will be granted;
I know not what will come to pass in our future days;
I hope only that good will come, my children, to you.

—Pawnee song

VENISON CABBAGE ROLLS

1 large head of cabbage	1/2 tsp. pepper
1 1/2 lbs. ground venison	1 cup cracker crumbs
1 egg	1/4 cup catsup
1/2 tsp. salt	1/4 cup butter, melted

Remove large leaves from cabbage. Trim off thick part of each leaf. Soak in boiling water for a few minutes so they become soft enough to roll. Combine burger, egg, salt, pepper, cracker crumbs and catsup. Place a mound of meat mixture in each leaf.

Fold over sides of each leaf and roll. Place in a Dutch oven with melted butter and cook over medium heat until browned. Then add enough water to cover the rolls. Bring to a boil. Then reduce heat and simmer for 1 hour. Take out cabbage rolls and make gravy using flour and spice to taste. Serve rolls covered with gravy.

VENISON POT ROAST WITH WILD CRANBERRIES

3 lb. venison roast	1/2 cup diced celery
Flour	6 sprigs parsley
2 tbsp. fat	1 large bay leaf
3 cups boiling water	2 whole cloves
2 cups raw cranberries	1 1/2 tsp. salt
1/2 cup diced onions	

Wash meat, pat dry. Sprinkle meat with a little flour and then brown on all sides in heated fat. Add all the remaining ingredients except salt. Cover and bring to a boil, then simmer for 2 1/2 hours. Add salt and turn meat over in gravy. If necessary, thicken gravy before serving. Serves 6.

QUICK MEAT PIE

1 can (10 oz.) tomato soup
3/4 cup water
1/4 tsp. rosemary
1/8 tsp. pepper
1 tsp. garlic powder
2 cups cooked, cubed venison
1 medium onion, chopped

1 can (16 oz.) whole potatoes, drained
1 can (16 oz.) diced carrots, drained
1/2 cup cheddar cheese
Pastry for 1 pie crust

Combine tomato soup and water and add the rosemary, pepper and garlic powder. Mix in cubed venison, onion, potatoes and carrots. Pour mixture into an ungreased baking dish and mix in cheese. Cover with pastry and seal at edges. Make two slits in center of pastry to allow steam to escape. Bake at 425°F for 20 minutes.

VENISON AND NOODLES

3/4 lb. lean venison steak, cut into thin strips
1 tbsp. margarine
1/2 cup chopped onion
1/4 tsp. pepper
1 1/4 cups homemade beef broth

1/4 cup lemon juice
1/4 tsp. cloves
1/3 cup gingersnap crumbs
1 tbsp. brown sugar
4 1/2 cups broad egg noodles
2 tbsp. margarine
2 tsp. poppy seeds

In a large skillet brown steak in the 1 tablespoon margarine. Add onion and pepper and cook until onion is tender. Add broth and lemon juice. Stir and add cloves. Bring to a boil and stir in gingersnap crumbs and brown sugar.

Simmer, uncovered, for 10 to 20 minutes or until sauce thickens. Meanwhile, cook noodles as directed on package. Drain. Toss hot noodles with the 2 tablespoons of margarine and the poppy seeds. Pour meat mixture over noodles and serve.

VENISON AND WILD RICE STEW

3 1/2 lbs. shoulder of venison, cut in 2-inch cubes
2 tsp. salt
1/8 tsp. fresh ground pepper

2 onions, peeled and quartered
1 1/2 cups wild rice, washed
2 qts. water

Place the venison, water and onions in a large heavy kettle and simmer, uncovered, for 3 hours, or until venison is tender. Mix in other ingredients, then simmer uncovered for about 30 minutes more until rice is tender. Stir frequently. Serve with fried bread and honey.

SPICED VENISON POT ROAST

4 tsp. whole cloves
4 tsp. allspice
1/4 tsp. whole black
    peppercorns
1 tsp. salt
1/2 tsp. ground nutmeg

1/2 tsp. ground mace
A 3 to 4-lb venison roast
2 tbsp. brown sugar
2 tbsp. vinegar
2 tbsp. lard
1/4 cup flour

Coarsely crack cloves, allspice and peppercorns. Mix with salt, nutmeg and mace. Rub spices over meat and press in. Place meat in a shallow dish. Combine sugar, vinegar and 1/4 cup water. Pour over meat and refrigerate overnight. Turn meat often. Remove meat and reserve the marinade. In a Dutch oven, brown meat in hot lard.

Add marinade and 1/2 cup of water. Cover and cook until tender, approx. 2 hours. Add more water if needed. Remove meat to warm platter and strain the juices, remembering to skim off fat. Add water to make 1 1/2 cups of fluid. Slowly blend 1/2 cup cold water into the flour. Stir into juices. Cook and stir until think. Cook 1 minute more. Season to taste. Serve sauce with roast.

BRAISED VENISON WITH VEGETABLES

2 lbs. steak, cut about 1 inch
    thick
1 tsp. salt
1/4 tsp. pepper
Flour

1/4 cup corn oil
2 cups tomato juice
1 can (12-20 oz.) whole kernel
    corn
1 can (12-20 oz) green beans

Cut meat into 6 serving pieces. Sprinkle with salt and pepper and dredge in flour. Brown meat in hot corn oil over medium heat. Pour tomato juice over meat. Cover and simmer for 45 minutes. Add vegetables and simmer for 15 minutes longer. Makes 6 servings.

VENISON-STUFFED PEPPERS

6 green peppers
2 1/2 cups cooked venison
6 mushrooms, sliced
2 scallions, sliced

1 tsp. salt
1/4 tsp. pepper
1/4 cup bacon drippings

Wash and core peppers. Saute remaining ingredients in bacon drippings. Stuff peppers with venison mixture and bake at 350°F for 45 minutes.

VENISON MINCEMEAT

1 quart apple cider
2 cups seedless raisins
1 cup dried cooked currants
3 greening apples, peeled,
    cored and chopped
1 cup chopped suet
2 lbs. ground venison

2 tsp. salt
2 tsp. cinnamon
2 tsp. ginger
1 tsp. cloves
1 tsp. nutmeg
1/2 tsp. allspice

Place the cider, raisins, currants, apples, and suet in a large heavy kettle. Cover, and simmer for 2 hours. Stir in remaining ingredients and simmer, uncovered, for 2 hours, stirring occasionally. Use as pie filling.

FRIED OR BOILED INDIAN SAUSAGE

Use tripe (boiled previously) inside out, about half a foot in length. Fill this with dried meat and grease, and fry until it is crisp. Then slice into pieces to serve.

TRIPE SAUSAGE SPECIAL

Select the straight intestine of a cow. With the two ends open, turn the intestine inside out. Place cubes of fresh venison, salt and pepper and seasoning in the tube. Fasten each end of the intestine with string. Boil the sausage for an hour; then it is ready to serve.

PUEBLO VENISON STEW

2 lbs. venison
Flour
1/4 cup oil
1 large onion, chopped
2 cloves garlic, minced
1 green pepper, chopped

1 cup dry corn kernels
1 cup pinto beans
1/2 cup pinon nuts
1/4 cup sunflower seeds
8 juniper berries
Salt and pepper to taste

Cut venison into 1" cubes, dredge venison in flour, brown in oil in heavy kettle. Transfer to a plate. Saute onion, garlic, and pepper in oil until onion is translucent.

Return meat to pan with remaining ingredients. Add enough water to cover venison. Simmer 3 hours or until tender.

VENISON STEAK

4 venison steaks
2 cups apple cider
1 cup white vinegar
2 carrots, sliced
2 onions, chopped
2 shallots, chopped

1 clove garlic, minced
2 bay leaves
1/4 tsp. pepper
1/8 tsp. thyme
1/2 cup oil

Marinate steaks, cut 1/2" to 3/4" thick, in a marinade made of remaining ingredients (except oil) for 24 hours. Remove steaks from marinade and pat dry.

Put marinade in small saucepan and cook it and vegetables until tender and sauce equals approximately 1/2 cup. Saute the steaks in shallow, hot fat until brown on both sides. Steaks will be rare. Serve sauce over steak.

BAKED VENISON HEART

1 3/4 lb. venison heart
1 1/2 tbsp. melted butter
2 cups soft bread crumbs
1 tbsp. finely chopped onion
1/4 tsp. salt

dash of pepper
1/2 tsp. sage
2 tbsp. shortening
1 1/2 cup boiling water

Wash heart in warm water to remove blood. Combine butter, bread crumbs, onion, and seasons and stuff heart. Skewer together. Sear in hot shortening, until browned on all sides.

Place on rack in roaster: add boiling water and also drippings from searing. Cover and bake at 325°F for 2 1/2 hours.

The true name of the Hurons is Wendat, "Dwellers of the Peninsula." Huron was a demeaning nickname given to them by European traders. It is from the French hure, *which means "ruffian."*

SWEET-AND-SOUR VENISON MEATBALLS

1 lb. ground venison
1 lb. ground pork
2 cups bread crumbs
2 eggs

1/2 cup chopped onion
2 tbsp. chopped parsley
1 small green pepper, chopped

SAUCE:

1 jar (10 oz.) apricot or peach
    jam

1/2 cup barbecue sauce

Combine venison, pork, bread crumbs, eggs, onion, parsley and green pepper. Form into balls and place 1 inch apart on cookie sheet. Bake at 325°F for 30 minutes.

Mix jam and barbeque sauce and pour over meatballs. Bake in 350°F oven for 30 minutes longer. Makes 4 to 5 dozen. Can be served as an appetizer or may be served as a main course.

UPSIDE-DOWN BURGER PIE

3/4 lb. ground venison
1 small onion, chopped
1 can (10 oz.) tomato soup
1 1/2 cups flour

1 tbsp. baking powder
1 tsp. salt
1/4 cup shortening
2/3 cup milk

Saute ground venison and onion until meat is browned. Drain. Add soup, place mixture in pie plate and set aside. Combine dry ingredients and cut in shortening. Mix in the milk, all at once. Knead until smooth. Roll out on a floured board in a circle large enough to cover the pie plate. Cover filling with pie crust and bake at 375°F for 15 to 20 minutes or until done.

VENISON OVEN STEW

2 lbs. cubed venison
1 can (28 oz.) tomatoes
1 small can mushrooms and
    liquid
2 medium onions, diced

1 can (10 oz.) tomato soup
1/2 soup can of water
Sale and pepper
Pinch of garlic
6 to 8 potatoes

Stir all ingredients, except potatoes together in a small roasting pan. Cover and cook for 1 1/2 hours at 350°F. Add potatoes and cook for 20 to 30 minutes longer.

BUFFALO

The buffalo was the mainstay of the Plains Indians, providing food, clothing, tools and shelter. It was also their meat of choice. Cooked much as we now cook beef, it was roasted, stewed, or dried and its bones formed the basis of soups. The buffalo and the buffalo hunt are prominent features of many ceremonies and religious beliefs. One of the most important celebrations was the Feast of the First Buffalo. As a matter of government policy, almost all were destroyed in the process of bringing the tribes into submission and relegating them to reservations.

THE MANY USES OF THE BUFFALO

PART	USE
Bones	Hide scraper
Small bones	Needles
Horn	Spoon
Muscle	Bow string
Hide	Moccasins
Stomach	Kettle
Nose bone	Paint brush
Tallow	Cooking oil
Bones	Arrow points
Shoulder blade	Digging tool
Skull	Bowl
Leg bone	Berry pounder

The most important tools used on the buffalo were the scraper, the flesher, and the drawsblade.

The scraper was a flat stone that was used to remove the meat and fat from the inside of the hide.

The flesher was a piece of flint with a handle. It was used to hack down the hide to the required thickness.

The drawsblade was a curved willow stick filled with a bone splinter. It was used to shave the hair from the hide.

TANNING

Tanning the hide was considered women's work by the Indians. The brains and liver of the buffalo were mixed with soapweed and grease and rubbed into both sides of the hide. After this mixture was allowed to soak into the hide overnight, the hide was then dried by the sun.

BLACKFEET PEMMICAN

Buffalo, cut in thin strips, was dried for the winter in much the same way jerky was. The meat, once dried, was crushed into powder on flat rocks. Pemmican was used in soups, was mixed with crushed berries (usually cherries or buffalo berries) and melted fat, and was frequently carried in leather pouches on journeys.

5 cup dried meat (pemmican)	1/4 cup shortening
3 cups mashed berries	1/4 cup sugar

Mix ingredients together in large bowl and serve. Cinnamon may be added for extra flavor.

NOTE: Pemmican was a staple among the Plains Indians and probably was the idea from which mincemeat sprang. The Pueblos varied the process slightly by using venison rather than buffalo and by using apricots or dried wild plums in place of berries.

PLAINS INDIAN PEMMICAN

Grind chokeberries, pits included. Add same amount of dried buffalo meat, pounded or ground fine. Mix meat and chokeberries with melted buffalo tallow, enough to hold mixture together and form into flat patties. Dry, these patties may be carried on trips away from camp. They are very nutritious.

BUFFALO POZOLE

2 large onions, chopped	1 can hominy, drained
3/4 lb. mushrooms	1 can baby corn
2 tbsp. oil	1/4 cup chopped cilantro
1 lb. buffalo	5 dried red hot chilies
2 cans tomatillos	Salt and pepper

Saute onion and mushrooms in oil in large kettle for 20 minutes. Pour mixture out of pan and set aside. Stir in buffalo, fry until browned and crumbly. Add reserved onions and mushrooms along with remaining ingredients and simmer gently for 30 minutes. Chilies may be removed and discarded if desired.

BUFFALO STEW

2 lbs. buffalo
1/4 cup oil
2 large onions, chopped
2 cloves garlic, minced
8 cups water
2 cups dried corn
12 juniper berries

1 tsp. oregano
1 tsp. salt
1/4 tsp. pepper
3 carrots, sliced
2 potatoes, cubed
1 green pepper, sliced

Cut buffalo into 1 inch cubes and brown in oil. Remove to a plate and saute onions and garlic in meat oil. Return meat to pan and add water, corn, juniper berries, oregano, salt and pepper. Cook 2 hours or until meat is tender. Add vegetables and cook until done, approximately 30 minutes.

JERKY INFORMATION

- A 4-pound slab of meat produces 1 pound of jerky.
- Jerky is 75% protein.
- Recommended as a light source of protein for hiking and canoe trips.
- Nobody should go into the bush without it. It's a survival food and tastes delicious.
- Original jerky was rubbed down with salt and hung in tepees to smoke and dry.
- French explorers yanked and pulled at the meat while it was hanging to speed up the drying process, hence the translated name "Jerked Beef."
- To eat, simply chew like gum; keep going, the flavor improves.

"It is strange that the Americans should complain that the Indians kill buffalo. We kill buffalo...for food and clothing, and to make our lodges warm. They kill buffalo for what? Go through the country. See the thousands of carcasses rotting on the plains. All they take is his head or his horns to show they have killed a buffalo....You call us savages. What are they?"

—Sitting Bull, 1877

BUFFALO JERKY

1 pkg. instant meat marinade
1/4 tsp. onion powder
1/4 tsp. garlic powder
1/2 tsp. Tabasco sauce
1/2 tsp. liquid smoke

1/4 tsp. black pepper
1 3/4 cup cold water
1 1/2 - 2 lbs. buffalo meat in
   strips 6 inches x 1/2 inch x
   1/2 inch.

Mix together all ingredients except meat to make a marinade. Place meat in container and cover with marinade, piercing meat slices deeply with fork. Marinate overnight in a covered container in refrigerator. Remove meat strips, drain slightly and place on rack, making sure strips do no overlap. Place a cookie sheet under the rack in a 150° - 175°F oven and bake 3 to 3 1/2 hours.

Remove from oven; cool, and store in a covered container in fridge. These larger pieces are not dried long and will be soft. Meat must be refrigerated to protect from spoilage.

GREAT HUMPED BACK ROAST

3 - 5 lbs. chuck or brisket roast
Garlic slivers
Onion slivers (optional)
1 cup vinegar

Oil
2 cups strong black coffee
2 cups water
Salt and pepper to taste

Using a large knife, cut slits completely through the meat. Insert slivers of garlic down into the slits (Onion may be substituted if you don't care for garlic, or use both, if you like.) Pour vinegar over the meat, making sure it runs down into the slits. Refrigerate meat for 24 to 48 hours.

When ready to cook, place roast in a big, heavy pot and brown in oil until nearly burned on all sides. Pour coffee over the meat. Add the water and cover.

Simmer on top of stove for 4 - 6 hours. Season with salt and pepper approximately 20 minutes before serving. It's guaranteed to fall apart at the touch of a fork, no matter how tough yours originally was. The gravy may be thickened or just left as is.

"We are seeking for life ourselves with our feet. Life is what we ask for from the White Buffalo. That is why the dancers are told: 'Dance, dance hard.'"

—Sauk Fox White Buffalo Dance

BUFFALOAF

1 cup fine dry bread crumbs
1 tsp. salt
Dash pepper
1/2 tsp. fine herbs
1/4 tsp. nutmeg
3 eggs

1 cup milk
2 lbs. buffalo burger
1 cup shredded carrot
Finely chopped onion and
   celery, to taste
1/2 cup hickory - flavored catsup

Place in bowl bread crumbs, salt, pepper, herbs and nutmeg. Add eggs and milk and beat well. Let stand a few minutes.

Gently blend in burger, carrot, onion and celery. Spread evenly in a 9 x 13-inch pan; spread catsup evenly over the meat mixture.

Bake at 325°F for 1 hour or until done. Let stand about 5 minutes before cutting.

TUCKER'S STEW FOR AN ARMY

2 large-sized buffalo
Brown gravy (lots)

Salt and pepper to taste
2 rabbits (optional)

Cut buffalo into bit-sized pieces, (this will take about 2 months, so start early. Reserve the heads and tails because you will need something to store the pieces in.

After the buffalo is all cut up, put it in a large pot and add enough brown gravy to cover the meat. Vegetables, etc, may be added at this time to taste.

Cook stew over a kerosene fire about 4 weeks at 400°F. Periodically add water and stir. Season to taste.

    This will serve about 3,937 people. If more guests are expected, the 2 rabbits may be added, but do this only if necessary because most people do not like fine hare in their stew.

What are those we see moving in the dust?
This way coming from the herd;
Buffalo and calf!
Food they promise for the Children.

                                                   —Pawnee song

ELK (WAPITI)

The elk (the Shawnee Indian name is *Wapiti*) is the second largest antlered animal in North America after the moose. Bull elks stand about 60 inches high at the shoulder and typically weigh 600 - 800 pounds, with record breakers weighing 1,200 pounds plus. The cow is somewhat smaller, weighing in the vicinity of 450 - 600 pounds.

The range of the elk, truly a regal animal in appearance, has diminished over the years. Predominantly, elk are now found in areas of Manitoba and Saskatchewan, the Rocky Mountains, the northern Pacific coast and the Black Hills of South Dakota. The bugle call of a bull elk is never forgotten.

ELK STEW WITH ACORN DUMPLINGS

1 1/2 lbs. elk meat	2 bay leaves
4 pieces bacon, chopped	3 potatoes, diced
1 quart water	2 carrots, sliced
1 tsp. salt	1/4 cup acorn meal
1 onion, chopped	1/2 cup cold water

Cut meat into 1"-cubes and brown with bacon. Add the 1 quart of water, salt, onions, and bay leaves. Cover and simmer 2 hours or until meat is tender. Add potatoes and carrots and cook 30 minutes longer. Combine acorn meal with the 1/2 cup water and stir into simmering stew. Top with Acorn Dumplings:

DUMPLINGS

1/2 cup acorn meal	1 egg, beaten
1/2 cup whole wheat flour	2 tbsp. milk
1 1/2 tsp. baking powder	2 tbsp. oil

Combine dumpling ingredients and beat until smooth. Drop by spoonfuls in simmering stew. Cover and steam 12 to 15 minutes.

What shall the little ones make to be a symbol of courage? They said to one another

The tall Elk who stands firmly upon the earth,

Our grandfather, we shall make to be a symbol of courage.

—Osage Rite of Vigil

MADBEAR'S ELK STEW

12 dried wild turnips
1 lb. dried elk meat
2 cups rice

7 wild onions (dice green onion tops)
Salt and pepper to taste

Soak dried turnips for 1 hour, use a large kettle for the stew. Let the turnips and dried meat simmer for 2 hours. Then add the onions, green tops and rice. Add salt and pepper and season to taste.

Boil for 10 minutes, cover and then let the stew simmer for 5 minutes. The stew is then ready to serve.

SPICY ELK MEATBALLS

1 lb. ground elk meat
2 tbsp. chopped green pepper
1 tbsp. grated onion
1/2 tsp. garlic salt
1/2 tsp. celery salt
1/2 cup wild rice

2 cups tomato juice
1 tbsp. honey
1 tbsp. Worcestershire sauce
1/2 tsp. cinnamon
2 whole cloves

Combine meat, green pepper, onion, garlic salt and celery salt. Form into balls about 1 inch in diameter. Roll meatballs in raw rice. Heat remaining ingredients in large covered skillet.

Add meatballs, cover and simmer 50 to 60 minutes. Serve over additional cooked wild rice. Makes five servings.

SAVORY STEW OF ELK

3 lbs. elk
3 tbsp. bacon fat
2 onions, chopped
2 cloves garlic, minced
1 quart water
1 tsp. salt

1/4 tsp. pepper
1/2 tsp. oregano
5 potatoes, cubed
6 carrots, sliced
1 1/2 cup celery, chopped
1/2 lb. mushrooms, sliced

Cut elk into 1-inch cubes, brown in bacon fat and remove meat to plate. Saute onions and garlic in fat until translucent. Add water, salt, pepper, oregano and meat and cook 2 1/2 hours until venison is tender. Add vegetables and cook until vegetables are done.

WAPITI WILD RICE STEW

3 1/2 lbs. elk shoulder, cut into
   2-in. cubes
2 qts. water
2 onions, peeled and quartered

1 1/2 cups wild rice, washed
2 tsp. salt
1/8 tsp. fresh ground pepper

Place the meat, water and onions in a large, heavy kettle and simmer, uncovered, for 3 hours, or until tender.

Mix in other ingredients, then simmer uncovered for about 30 minutes more until rice is tender. Stir frequently. Serve with fried bread and honey.

MOOSE

The moose is the largest antlered mammal on earth, weighing as much as 1,800 lbs and being, on the average, 7 1/2 ft. tall to the shoulder. Moose are long legged and have a high hump - shaped body, which is dark brown in color. For their size, moose are very quiet animals with extremely well developed senses of smell and hearing. They spend a good deal of time in the water and are excellent swimmers, even over long distances.

The only threat to the moose, besides man, is the wolf. Only when the moose is in a very weakened condition can a wolf pack take advantage of this great animal. The moose is a territorial animal, rarely leaving its 5 square-mile range except perhaps in the mating season.

The moose's diet consists of foliage, grasses and aquatic plants. Moose meat is highly recommended as a substitute for many other red meats.

The moose is called *moos* by the Algonquin tribes, *mos* by the Delawares and *monswa* by the Cree — all mean *he who strips off*, referring to the eating method characteristic of the moose.

CURRIED MOOSE BURGERS

1 lb. ground moose
1/4 cup bacon drippings
1 small can tomato sauce

2 onions, chopped
1/2 tsp. horseradish
1 1/2 tsp. curry powder

Shape meat into patties. Fry in bacon drippings, over medium heat, until brown on both sides. Stir in remaining ingredients; cover and simmer for 5 minutes or until meat is well done. Turn meat once.

MOOSE PEMMICAN

1 lb. moose meat, well trimmed
1/2 cup raisins
3 dates
2 tbsp. melted suet

2 tbsp. melted vegetable
    shortening
1 tbsp. lemon juice

Cut meat into thin slices and dry as for jerky in a slow oven (175° - 200°F) for 4 to 5 hours. Put the dried meat through a coarse grinder, then pulverize it into a fine powder. Grind the raisins and dates together and work into the meat with a fork or fingers until thoroughly blended.

Combine the melted suet, shortening and lemon juice. Pour over the meat/fruit until the mixture will hold together. Shape into small patties. The Indian pemmican patty was about 3 inches in diameter and 1/2 inch thick.

This is nourishing and keeps without refrigeration.

MOOSE STEAKS WITH RICE

2 tbsp. lard
1 lb. moose, cut into thin strips
2 onions, sliced
1 clove garlic, chopped
1/2 cup chopped celery
Salt and pepper to taste

1 cup water
2 tsp. cornstarch
1/4 cup water
1 tsp. soy sauce

Melt lard and slowly brown moose strips over low heat. Add onion, garlic, and celery. Season with salt and pepper. Add the 1 cup water and simmer, covered for 20 minutes. Thicken with cornstarch, the 1/4 cup of water and soy sauce. Simmer for 5 minutes longer. Serve hot over boiled rice.

"Redskin" was a term invented by the English to refer to the Algonquin tribes. It wasn't for the color of their skin, though. It referred to the vermilion makeup that the both the men and women always wore.

SPANISH MOOSE STEAK

1/4 cup flour
1/2 tsp. salt
1/2 tsp. pepper
2 lbs. moose, caribou or bear
    steak
2 tbsp. fat

1 green pepper, chopped
1 clove garlic, chopped
6 small onions, sliced
1 cup tomatoes
1 cup peas

Season flour with salt and pepper. Dredge meat with seasoned flour. Brown meat on both sides in hot fat; remove from pan.

Saute green pepper and garlic in same fat until tender. Place pepper and garlic over meat. Place meat in pan; add onions and tomatoes. Simmer until tender; approx. 2 hours.

Shortly before the meat is cooked, add peas and more seasoning if necessary. Arrange on a platter with vegetables on top.

MOOSE STEAK WITH MUSHROOM SAUCE

3 tbsp. bacon drippings
1 large moose steak
1/2 cup bouillon or consomme
1 medium onion, chopped
1/2 tsp. garlic powder
3 tbsp. tomato paste

1/2 cup water or sherry
1 cup sliced mushrooms
2 tbsp. flour
1/4 cup cream
Dash of paprika

Heat bacon drippings in large skillet and brown steak on both sides thoroughly. Add broth, onion, garlic powder and tomato paste diluted in the 1/2 cup of water or sherry. Cover pan and simmer for 1 hour or until meat is tender. Remove steak from pan and keep hot. Add mushrooms to pan liquid; cover and simmer for 1 minute. Mix flour with enough water to form a paste. Use to thicken pan liquid. Dilute with cream. Heat thoroughly.

Taste for seasoning. Pour over steak and sprinkle with paprika.

WHITNEY POT ROAST

This recipe comes from Ontario, Canada, just outside magnificent Algonquin National Park.

4 lbs. moose steaks, 1/2 lb. each
Salt, pepper and paprika
1/2 cup butter or oil
4 large onions, sliced
2 garlic cloves, minced
1/2 cup wine vinegar

1 small can tomato paste and an equal amount of water
1 tbsp. pickling spice, tied in a bag
3 bay leaves
Flour and water paste

Place steaks in cold water overnight. The next day, pat dry, and season with salt, pepper and paprika. In a skillet, quickly brown steaks in butter or oil. Remove meat from skillet and set aside. Saute onion and garlic until transparent and add remaining ingredients. Place meat in a heavy roast pan and pour onion mixture over it. Cover and cook in a 350°F oven for 2 hours or until meat is tender. Remove spice bag and bay leaves. Thicken liquid with flour and water paste. Serve.

MOOSE AND CABBAGE TURNOVERS

3 tbsp. butter
3/4 cup finely chopped onion
1 1/2 lbs. ground moose
4 cups grated cabbage
3/4 cup grated raw carrot
2 tsp. salt
1/4 tsp. pepper

1/4 tsp. mace
1/4 tsp. Worcestershire sauce
2 tbsp. water
Dough for a double crust pie
1 egg yolk
1 tbsp. water

Heat butter in a large saucepan. Add onions and cook gently until tender, about 5 minutes. Add meat and stir until all redness disappears. Add cabbage, carrots, salt, pepper, mace, Worcestershire sauce and water. Cover and simmer for 15 minutes.

Uncover and continue cooking until the liquid cooks away. Meat should be moist but not wet. Cool.

Roll out pastry and cut into 6-inch squares. Put 1/4 cup of meat mixture on each square. Moisten adjacent edges and fold over (in a triangle shape). Press edges together. Prick with a fork. Place on large cookie sheet or sheets. Beat egg yolk and water together and brush over tops of turnovers. Bake for 25 to 30 minutes, or until very well browned. Serve at once.

DEEP DISH MOOSE PIE

1/2 cup flour
1 tsp. salt
2 lbs. moose meat, cubed
3 carrots, peeled and sliced
2 onions, chopped

1 cup turnips, cubed
5 medium potatoes, cubed
3 tbsp. cornstarch
pastry for a single-crust pie

Combine the flour and salt; dredge cubed meat. Then brown meat in an oiled skillet. Add 4 cups of water and simmer for 2 hours. Add carrots, onions and turnips; when tender, add potatoes. Add more water if necessary. Thicken with cornstarch and water. Pour into a baking dish. Cover with the pastry; make 2 slits in the center and bake at 350°F for 20 to 25 minutes.

MOOSE CHEESE LOAF

2 lbs. ground moose meat
1 large onion, chopped
1 large green pepper, chopped
1 cup dry bread crumbs
1 1/2 cups diced cheese

2 1/2 cups milk
2 tsp. salt
1 tsp. pepper
1 tsp. celery salt
1 tsp. paprika

Combine all ingredients and mix thoroughly. Place into greased loaf pans and bake at 350°F for 2 hours.

STUFFED PEPPER MOOSE STEAK

1 large moose steak
1/4 cup flour

1/2 tsp. salt
1/4 tsp. pepper

STUFFING:

3 cups bread crumbs
3/4 cup chopped celery
3/4 cup chopped onion
1 sweet green pepper, sliced

1/2 cup butter
1/2 tsp. paprika
Salt and pepper

Combine stuffing ingredients and spread evenly over steak. Roll up and tie. Mix flour, salt and pepper together. Dredge steak roll with mixture. Set the roll in a greased roasting pan. Cover and bake at 350°F for 1 hour.

BEAR

The color of the black bear varies, from black to all shades of brown. Bears are found throughout all wooded areas of North America, and range in a radius of about 15 miles. They are ordinarily independent creatures. Man is their only threat.

Bears are very clean animals, grooming often. They tend to eat anything, from ants to elk and all kinds of vegetation. Generally, they weigh in at 200 - 300 lbs, and the meat of the young bear is delicious.

The bear is skinned and butchered much the same as the domestic cow. It is important that the pelt not be marred during the process, because of its value.

ROAST BEAR

3 lbs. bear roast
2 cups water

1 can pineapple slices, and juice
3 large onions

Place roast in pan. Pour water over meat; then cover with pineapple slices reserving juice. Slice onions and place alongside roast.

Cover roast with aluminum foil and bake for 1 hour. Add juice from pineapple to roast and continue cooking for 1 1/2 hours.

BEAR CHOPS

6 medium bear chops
1 clove garlic, halved
2 tbsp. bacon fat
1 large onion, chopped
4 cooked carrots, diced

1/4 cup flour
4 tbsp. chili sauce
1/2 cup dry wine
Salt and pepper to taste

Rub chops with halved clove of garlic. Melt bacon fat in a skillet and sear chops on both sides. Place the chops in a lightly greased baking dish. Saute the onions and carrots in skillet until onions are transparent. Mix in flour, chili sauce and wine. Cook until thickened. On top of each chop place equal amounts of carrot mixture. Pour 1 cup of water into the baking dish season with salt and pepper. Cover with tin foil and bake at 375°F for 60 to 70 minutes or until tender.

ROAST BEAR IN RAISIN SAUCE

A 3 - to 4 - lb bear roast
3 1/2 cups water
1 tbsp. flour
1 1/2 tsp. dry mustard

1/2 tsp. salt
1/4 tsp. pepper
2 tbsp. lemon juice
1/4 cup seedless raisins

Cut all fat from roast; place in a roasting pan and pour in 2 cups of the water. Cover and roast for 2 1/2 hours at 350°F. Mix flour, mustard, salt and pepper in a saucepan. Slowly mix in remaining water and lemon juice. Add raisins. Cook over medium heat, stirring constantly until sauce reaches consistency of syrup. Pour over bear roast and continue to roast for 30 minutes, basting 2 to 3 times throughout the baking time.

Don't forget to check Chapter 7 for more special sauces and marinades.

SPICED BEAR ROAST

8 medium onions, sliced
3 tbsp. bacon fat
Salt, pepper and garlic powder
1/4 cup prepared mustard

3/4 cup catsup
1/3 cup flour
3 cups boiling water

Saute onions in bacon fat and spread evenly on bottom of a roast pan. Trim bear roast of all fat; wash and place in roast pan. Sprinkle with salt, pepper and garlic powder. Combine mustard and catsup and spread thickly over the roast. Roast at 350°F for 3 1/2 to 4 hours, basting frequently. Transfer meat to a hot platter and skim fat from drippings. Stir in flour until all the flour disappears and add the 3 cups of boiling water. Cook and stir until thick for gravy.

BEAR POT ROAST

A 3-lb. bear roast
Flour
1/2 tsp. salt
1/4 tsp. pepper

1/2 tsp. cinnamon
Garlic to taste
1 cup water
1/2 cup sherry wine
3 tbsp. white vinegar

Wipe roast dry and rub well with flour. Sprinkle on salt, pepper, cinnamon and garlic. Place roast in a roasting pan. Add water, wine and vinegar. Cover and bake at 375°F, allowing 25 to 30 minutes per pound.

SWEET BEAR ROAST

1/2 cup pineapple juice or
    vinegar
3 tbsp. brown sugar
1 tbsp. dry mustard
1/2 cup catsup

A 3 - to 4 - lb. roast
2 cups water

Mix pineapple juice or vinegar, brown sugar, dry mustard and catsup together in a large bowl. Place roast into mix and cover the meat completely with the marinade. Cover and let stand in refrigerator for 10 to 12 hours, turning occasionally. Remove roast from marinade and place in a roasting pan. Add the 2 cups of water and the marinade to the pan.

Cover and roast at 350°F for 3 1/2 to 4 hours, basting occasionally.

PAN-FRIED BEAR STEAK

4 bear steaks, 1 inch thick
1 onion, sliced
1/2 cup vinegar
1/2 cup vegetable oil
1/2 cup water

1 tbsp. pickling spice
1 tbsp. salt
1 tbsp. bacon fat
salt and pepper

Trim all fat from bear steak and wash in cold water. Place steaks in a glass bowl. Add onion, vinegar, oil, water, pickling spice and the tablespoon salt. Marinate for at least 24 hours in the refrigerator, turning frequently. Remove steaks, pat dry and fry over medium heat in a pan that has been rubbed with bacon fat or oil. To prevent sticking turn often until done. Add a little more fat when necessary. Add salt and pepper to taste. Marinade is optional. If used, bring to a boil, reduce heat and simmer 5 minutes. Pour over steak to serve.

"The leading ceremonial attendant cares for the pumpkins. It is said those are the ones the White Buffalo thinks of most when they are offered. Then the corn dumplings, then the meat: ducks, turkeys, grouse and all kinds of things that fly. Then those giving the festival offered deer and bear and elk. But the corn and the pumpkins, these are handled with greatest care."

—from the Sauk Fox festival for the White Buffalo

BRAISED BEAR STEAK

A 2 - lb. bear steak
Bacon fat
2 large onions, sliced
2 cans (10 oz. each) tomato
   soup

1 can water
2 tsp. lemon juice
1/2 tsp. salt
1/4 tsp. pepper
3/4 tsp. cinnamon

Pat steak dry. Brown meat on both sides in a large skillet with a small amount of bacon fat. Add onions, tomato soup, water and lemon juice. Sprinkle salt, pepper and cinnamon over meat. Cover and simmer for 1 1/2 to 2 hours, turning occasionally.

BARBECUED BEAR STEAK

2 lbs. bear steak
3 tbsp. butter or margarine
1 slice salt pork, cut up
1 onion, sliced
1 cup catsup

1/3 cup steak sauce
2 tbsp. vinegar
1 tbsp. lemon juice
1 tsp. salt
1 tbsp. chili powder

Trim all fat from bear steak and cut into 2 - inch cubes. Put butter or margarine in a heavy frying pan; sear meat on all sides, along with salt pork. Place meat in a casserole dish. Cover with onion.

Add the rest of the ingredients to frying pan and bring to a boil, stirring constantly. Pour sauce over meat and onions in casserole.

Cover and bake at 325°F until tender, approximately 2 hours.

✳ CHAPTER TWO ✳
SMALL GAME

Dress all game as soon as possible to ensure freshness and to prevent bacterial growth.

If the intestines have been shot up, and their contents have gotten onto the flesh, they must be carefully cut out and their contents wiped away.

Look for any yellowish fatty kernels under each front shoulder and the small of the back. If these are not removed, the meat will have an unpleasant taste.

Old and tough animals may required parboiling for tenderness.

RABBITS AND HARES

Although there are different types of rabbits and hares, they all have certain things in common: long ears; long, powerful hind legs and great speed. Most are grayish to brown on top and white underneath. The common snowshoe rabbit changes to white all over during the winter months. Depending on the type of animal, the weight varies from 2 to 8 lbs.

All rabbits and hares are vegetarians. They can be found in all parts of North America.

Rabbits and hares are an excellent table meat, as can be seen by the number of domestic rabbit breeders found today.

In the Smoky Mountains, near the western border of Tennesee, there is a peak called Tsistu'yi by the Cherokee. It is the "Rabbit Place" where the chief of the rabbits, who was as large as a deer and ruled over all the smaller rabbits, lived. In old times, it is said, the people could go there and see him.

TAOS RABBIT

1 medium rabbit
2 tbsp. oil
1 onion, chopped
1 tbsp. red chili powder

1 tsp. salt
1 cup vinegar
2 quarts water
1/2 cup cornmeal

Cut rabbit into serving pieces, place oil in large saucepan and brown rabbit in oil. Add remaining ingredients (except cornmeal) and simmer for 1 1/2 hours or until meat is tender. Add cornmeal gradually to pan, blending thoroughly. Simmer 10 minutes until the sauce thickens.

STEWED WILD RABBIT

5 lbs. wild rabbit
1/4 tsp. pepper
1 1/2 cup flour
3/4 cup oil

2 quarts water
2 tsp. salt
12 boiling onions
8 carrots, sliced

DUMPLINGS:

2 cups flour
1 tbsp. baking powder
1/2 tsp. salt

1 tbsp. oil
1 cup milk

Cut rabbit into serving pieces, sprinkle with pepper. Dredge in flour and brown in oil. Drain off oil, add water and salt, and simmer, covered, for 2 hours. Add vegetables; simmer 1 hour.

Combine dry ingredients for dumplings; add oil and milk and stir. Drop dumplings into boiling stew broth, cover, cook 10 to 12 minutes.

RABBIT DELIGHT

1 young rabbit
1 tbsp. fat
1/2 cup mushrooms, chopped
2 green peppers, chopped
1 cup broth, or 1 cup water plus
    1 chicken bouillon cube

1/4 cup lemon juice
3/4 cup orange juice
1/2 tsp. salt
1/4 tsp. pepper
Pinch of ginger
1 tbsp. chopped parsley

Cut up the rabbit and brown pieces in fat in a heavy pot. Add mushrooms, green peppers, broth and other liquids; season with salt, pepper, ginger and parsley. Cover and cook slowly until tender.

RABBIT 'N' GRAVY

1 onion, sliced
1 tbsp. dry mustard
1 1/2 cups cider vinegar
2 tsp. salt
1/2 tsp. pepper

2 rabbits, cut into serving pieces
1 1/2 cups all purpose flour
1/4 tsp. ground nutmeg
1 tsp. sugar
Clear bacon fat

Combine onion, mustard, vinegar, salt and pepper. Drop in rabbit pieces, covering pieces completely. Let stand for 1 hour, turning rabbit occasionally.

Mix 1 cup of flour with nutmeg and sugar in a paper bag. Drain rabbit pieces then put a few pieces at a time in the bag and shake well. Put enough bacon fat in a skillet to brown rabbit pieces.

When all have been browned, remove meat and pour off all but 1/2 cup fat. Stir in 1/2 cup flour. Gradually stir in 3 cups of boiling water. Simmer, stirring constantly till thickened. Arrange rabbit pieces in gravy; cover and simmer for 1 1/2 to 2 hours.

RABBIT HOT POT CASSEROLE

1 wild rabbit, dressed
4 carrots, peeled and sliced
4 potatoes, peeled and sliced

1 package onion soup mix
2 1/2 cups hot water

Cut rabbit into serving pieces and wash well. Blanch rabbit by putting it into a saucepan, covering it with water bringing the water to a boil. Remove rabbit from saucepan and place in a greased casserole dish. Cover rabbit with the carrots and potatoes. Mix soup with the hot water and pour over vegetables. Cover and bake at 350°F for 2 hours.

CURRIED RABBIT

1 rabbit, cut into serving pieces
Flour
3 tbsp. bacon drippings
2 onions, chopped
1 tbsp. curry powder

Dash cayenne
3 tbsp. warm water
1 cup stock
2 apples, peeled and sliced

Dredge meat pieces with flour and brown in bacon drippings. Remove rabbit. In same pan, saute onions. In a cup, mix together curry powder, cayenne and warm water to make a paste. Spread paste over rabbit pieces and return rabbit to pan with sauteed onions. Pour stock over, stir and cover. Simmer for 20 minutes. Add apple slices and continue to simmer for 15 minutes.

STEWED RABBIT

3 tbsp. cooking oil
1/2 lb. bacon, chopped
6 bay leaves
1 cup finely chopped onion
1 clove garlic, crushed
1/4 tsp. pepper
1/4 cup tomato paste
4 cups stewed tomatoes
1/4 tsp. red pepper
1/2 tsp. oregano
1/4 cup margarine
1 tbsp. chopped parsley
1/2 tsp. salt
1 rabbit, cut in serving pieces
Flour
1/2 cup dry red wine

Heat oil over medium heat in a deep saucepan. Add bacon and bay leaves to hot oil. Add onions and saute till golden brown. Add crushed garlic clove and pepper to pot and cook until mixture is well browned. Add tomato paste, stewed tomatoes, red pepper, oregano, margarine, parsley and salt. Bring mixture to a boil; remove from heat.

Dredge rabbit sections with flour and brown in a hot skillet. When meat is brown add red wine. Simmer for 5 minutes, then add rabbit and wine to the saucepan. Return to heat and simmer rabbit and sauce for 20 minutes.

Serve with rice or noodles.

BAKED STUFFED RABBIT

1 rabbit
2 large carrots, quartered
4 strips bacon or salt pork
1 to 2 cups hot water

STUFFING:

2 cups mashed potatoes
2 stalks celery, chopped
1 tbsp. butter
Pinch of salt, pepper, and savory

Skin and clean rabbit; wash with warm salted water. Mix stuffing ingredients; fill body of rabbit with stuffing and sew it up.

Place rabbit breast-down on rack of baking pan, with legs folded under the body and fastened in this position. Place quartered carrots beside it on the rack. Fasten strips of bacon or pork over back of rabbit with toothpicks to keep the flesh from drying out.

Place pan in a 400°F oven for 10 minutes; then pour a cup or two of the hot water over meat and continue until tender, about 1 hour. Remove bacon for the last 10 minutes and let the rabbit brown.

POT ROAST OF RABBIT

Rabbit, cut into serving pieces
Milk

Flour
Oil

Dip rabbit in milk, then coat with flour. Fry in hot oil until browned. Pour off excess oil from pan.

SAUCE:

2 tbsp. melted butter
2 onions, chopped
1 clove garlic, crushed
1 tbsp. parsley flakes

Pinch of thyme
3 1/2 cups tomato juice
1 tsp. Worcestershire sauce
Salt and pepper

Mix together all ingredients for sauce and pour over rabbit. Simmer, covered, for 1 1/2 hours.

RABBIT-HAM CROQUETTES

2 tbsp. butter or margarine
2 1/2 tbsp. flour
Dash dry mustard
3/4 cup milk
1 tsp. onion juice or grated
    onion
2/3 cup ground cooked ham

1 1/3 cups chopped cooked
    rabbit meat
1 tsp. chopped parsley
1 tsp. chopped green pepper
1 egg, beaten
3 cups fine dry bread crumbs

Melt butter or margarine and stir in flour and mustard. Cook until mixture bubbles. Add milk gradually, stirring constantly. Add onion and cook over low heat until sauce is thick and smooth, stirring occasionally. Add ham, rabbit, parsley and green pepper. Cool. If mixture is very soft, chill it until it is firm enough to handle easily.

Shape into eight croquettes. Dip them in the beaten egg, then roll them in bread crumbs. Fry croquettes in deep fat, 360°F, for about 4 minutes, or until golden brown.

"To appeal for aid in planting the fields, rise with the sun...paint the parting of your hair red for this work. The red line represents the path of the God of the Day and will make the paths of all the animals converge toward you, for upon them you and your children must depend."

—*Osage Rite of Vigil*

PARMESAN RABBIT

1 rabbit
1/2 cup bread crumbs
1/2 cup Parmesan cheese
1 egg

Salt and pepper
1/4 lb. butter
1/2 cup tomato juice

Cut rabbit into generous serving pieces. Flatten by pounding meat gently. In a bowl, mix bread crumbs and Parmesan cheese together. In another bowl, beat an egg with salt and pepper.

Roll pieces of meat in crumbs, then in the beaten egg and then again in crumb mixture. Fry in butter over medium heat for 30 minutes. Add tomato juice and cook for another hour over very low heat.

CRABAPPLE RABBIT ROAST

1 rabbit, dressed
1 lemon, halved
1 clove garlic
1 tsp. salt
1 tsp. pepper

1 1/2 tsp. summer savory
2 tbsp. crabapple jelly
2 strips bacon
1 tbsp. parsley
1 pint crabapples

Wash rabbit and pat dry. Rub inside and outside of rabbit well with lemon halves. Then rub well with garlic clove. Sprinkle cavity with salt, pepper and savory. Coat breast with crabapple jelly and cover with bacon strips. Place rabbit in a small roasting pan: cover and bake at 350°F for 1 1/2 hours.

To serve, garnish with parsley and whole preserved crabapples.

ROAST RABBIT

2 cups dried bread crumbs
1/2 lb. sausage meat
1 tbsp. chopped parsley
1 tbsp. diced onion

Salt and pepper
1 rabbit, dressed
Oil or fat

Combine bread crumbs, sausage meat, parsley, onion, salt and pepper. Wash rabbit and pat dry. Stuff cavity with bread crumb mixture and sew it closed. Rub rabbit with oil or fat. Place in roasting pan, add 1 cup of water and roast uncovered at 325°F for 1 1/2 to 2 hours.

RABBIT STEW AND SLAP JACKS

1 wild rabbit
1 tsp. salt
1/2 tsp. pepper
1 medium onion, chopped

4 carrots, sliced
2 cups diced turnip
4 potatoes, diced
2 tbsp. flour or cornstarch

Parboil rabbit for 40 minutes and drain. Then cover with water; add salt and pepper, then bring to a boil. Add vegetables and cook for 1 hour. Thicken broth with flour or cornstarch. Add more water when necessary.

SLAP JACKS:

2 cups flour
1/2 tsp. salt
1/4 tsp. pepper

1/4 tsp. sage
3/4 cup water

Combine flour and seasonings for slap jacks. Make a well; then add the water, stirring as you pour. Turn out onto a floured board and knead a few times. Roll out to 1/2 inch thickness and cut into squares. Add to boiling stew and cover. Cook for 15 to 20 minutes.

SWEET AND SOUR RABBIT

1/4 cup margarine
2 to 3 lbs. rabbit, cut-up
1 1/2 tsp. salt
1/4 tsp. pepper
1 cup pineapple juice
1/2 cup vinegar

1 cup pineapple chunks
1 medium green pepper
1/4 cup sugar
1 1/2 tsp. cornstarch
1/2 cup water

Heat margarine in a skillet and brown rabbit pieces over medium heat. Sprinkle on salt and pepper. Add pineapple juice and vinegar. Cover and simmer for 45 minutes or until meat is tender.

Mix in pineapple chunks and green pepper. Simmer for 5 minutes. Mix sugar and cornstarch into the 1/2 cup water. Stir into the rabbit mixture. Simmer for 5 minutes. Serve.

RABBIT SOUP

Leftover rabbit meat and bones
1 soup bone
1/4 lb. salt pork
3 carrots, sliced
1 onion, quartered
1 clove garlic
1/4 tsp. chopped parsley

1/4 tsp. thyme
1 bay leaf
4 cups chicken broth
Salt and pepper
1 cup diced potatoes
1/2 cup diced celery
1/2 cup diced carrots

Remove all meat from rabbit bones and set meat aside. In a kettle, combine rabbit bones and soup bone and salt pork. Add sliced carrots, onion, garlic, parsley, thyme and bay leaf. Cover with water and simmer until almost dry.

Add chicken broth and simmer 15 minutes. Strain broth and adjust the seasoning to taste. Discard bones and seasoning vegetables.

Add potatoes to broth and simmer until tender. Add celery and carrots and cook 20 minutes longer. Add rabbit meat. Heat thoroughly and serve.

BEAVER

The beaver is a small game animal with a heavy body, short legs, large web feet and scaly tail. The fur is dense and varies from reddish chestnut to deep brown and almost black.

The average weight of a mature beaver is 40-50 lbs. In order to survive, it lives on tree bark, grasses and aquatic plants.

The beaver is an aquatic animal which, if necessary, creates its own water reservoir by use of dams. Beavers build houses out of sticks and mud; with water entrances, but tall enough to be above the water line. They are tireless workers and very docile. When alarmed, they slap their tails on the water as a warning. The major enemy of the beaver is man, but they sometimes fall prey to the larger predators, such as the wolf.

Beaver is an excellent table meat. Everyone should try beaver tails before they die.

BEAVER WITH STUFFING

Parboil 2 hind beaver quarters for 30 minutes and rinse. Repeat method twice. Make stuffing of your choice. In a roasting pan lay one hind quarter and cover with stuffing. Put remaining hind quarter on top and tie two together with string. Pour on 2 cups of water; cover and roast for 35 to 40 minutes, at 325°F.

Note: To determine parboiling time, the beaver is ready to put in the oven when it can be pierced easily.

"You shall have power to attain me, for I am called game animal, and I shall not fail to know when you desire me. When one of us is killed, he is not killed definitely but lives again. This is because we are unwilling for anyone to make a killing without thought, and he who kills without thought will not be blessed by us and will not obtain us."

—Sauk Fox tale

ROAST BEAVER

1 beaver, quartered
2 tbsp. pickling spice
2 tbsp. dry mustard
1/2 cup dry wine

1/2 cup brown sugar
1 cup pineapple juice
1 tsp. lemon juice
1/2 cup water

Parboil beaver quarters for 30 minutes and rinse. Repeat method twice. Place beaver quarters in a clean pot with enough water to cover; add pickling spice and boil for 20 minutes. Drain and rinse with warm water. Place meat in a roast pan. Combine dry mustard, dry wine, brown sugar, pineapple juice, lemon juice and water. Pour over meat and roast for 1 hour at 325°F, basting often.

BOILED BEAVER

Hind quarter of beaver
1 large onion

3 carrots, sliced
2 tsp. salt

Boil beaver for 1/2 hour. Drain and rinse. Repeat method twice. Cover with water again, then add remaining ingredients. Cover and boil until tender. Dispose of vegetables as they will hold most of the wild taste from the beaver.

BEAVER TAILS IN SAUCE

2 beaver tails
1/2 cup white vinegar
1 tsp. salt
2 tsp. baking soda
1/4 cup flour
1/2 tsp. salt
1/4 tsp. pepper

1/4 cup oil
1/4 cup cider vinegar
1 tsp. dry mustard
1 tsp. sugar
1/2 tsp. garlic powder
2 tbsp. Worcestershire sauce

The day before, skin the beaver tails. Cover tails in cold water and wash thoroughly. Rinse. Place tails in a pot and cover with cold water. Add the 1/2 cup white vinegar and the 1 teaspoon salt. Soak overnight. Drain.

Place tails in a heavy pot. Cover with water and add the baking soda. Cover and bring to a boil. Reduce heat and simmer for 12 to 15 minutes. Drain.

Combine flour, salt and pepper. Dredge beaver tails in the seasoned flour. Heat the oil in a skillet. Add beaver tails and saute over low heat until tender.

Combine the 1/4 cup cider, vinegar, mustard, sugar, garlic powder and Worcestershire sauce. Add to the skillet and simmer covered for 20 minutes, basting often.

GROUNDHOG, OR WOODCHUCK

The groundhog, also known as the woodchuck, is a small animal, weighing from 5 to 10 lbs. and generally having coarse brown fur. The groundhog lives in a burrow of its own making. This house has several tunnels and several emergency exits. Usually you will find three sleeping chambers at the end of the tunnel. Because of its low intelligence level, the animal is easily killed by man. The groundhog is known to be 90% vegetarian.

Groundhog is an excellent table meat that is easily found throughout the countryside in open grassy areas and farmer's fields. The hide, when tanned, is extremely durable.

COOKED GROUNDHOG

1 groundhog
Water
1 carrot, sliced

2 onions, sliced
2 potatoes, sliced
1 tsp. garlic

To clean a groundhog, you must first remove the insides. Make a fire outside and scorch hair from the groundhog. Use a sharp knife to scrape off all scorched hair. Wash and clean groundhog with cold water. Put in a large pot with enough water to cover and add all remaining ingredients. Boil until meat is tender, then dispose of vegetables. Refrigerate meat until the next day, when it will be best for eating. Can be reheated.

PRESSURE-COOKED GROUNDHOG

1 groundhog, dressed
Flour

Salt
Bacon fat

Note: Be sure to remove the kernel from behind the front legs to keep from spoiling the flavor of the meat.

Cut the groundhog into serving pieces and roll in flour. Sprinkle with salt; slightly brown the meat in bacon fat. Put the insert pan in pressure cooker with 1/2 inch of water on the bottom. Put in the meat pieces and cook for about 70 minutes with 15 pounds pressure.

ROAST GROUNDHOG

1 cup cooking oil
1/4 cup lemon juice
1 groundhog, dressed
3 cups bread crumbs

1 small onion, chopped fine
Salt and pepper to taste
1/2 cup evaporated milk
4 tsp. bacon fat

Combine oil and lemon juice and marinate groundhog in this overnight. Mix together bread crumbs, onion, salt and pepper. Mix in milk until well combined. Removed meat from the marinade and pat dry. Stuff bread crumb mixture into the groundhog and sew cavity closed. Brush with bacon fat and place in a roasting pan. Cover and roast at 300°F for 1 1/2 to 2 hours. You may need to add a little water.

FRIED WOODCHUCK

1 woodchuck
1 tbsp. salt
1 cup flour

1/2 tsp. salt
1/4 tsp. pepper
1/4 cup fat

Skin and clean woodchuck and cut into 6 or 7 pieces. Put in pot, add salt and enough water to cover, and parboil for 1 hour.

Remove meat from the broth, and drain. Dredge meat in flour, salt and pepper. Melt fat in heavy skillet and saute woodchuck until nicely browned.

"The pipe is us. The stem is our backbone, the bowl our head. The stone is our blood, red as our skin."

—a Sioux's description of the sacred pipes of the Plains people

MUSKRAT

The muskrat is a small animal that weights approximately 2 lbs. It is dark brown in color and light grey or tan through the belly. It adapts well to aquatic life because of its scaly flattened tail, and valves or flaps that keep water from its nose, mouth and ears.

Muskrat prefer to live in freshwater marshes and slow-moving streams. They are known to have several houses for dwelling and feeding. The food source for muskrat consists of cattails, bulrushes, submerged pond weed, crayfish and frogs.

Similar to the beaver, muskrat are active throughout the year. Many people consider muskrat a delicacy and look forward to the trapping season, when the meat is utilized as well as the hide.

BAKED MUSKRAT

2 muskrat, skinned and cleaned
1/2 cup flour
1/2 tsp. salt
1/4 tsp. pepper

1/4 tsp. sage
1/4 cup lemon juice
1/4 cup water
Bacon strips to cover (optional)

Boil meat for about 30 minutes; drain and rinse. Repeat. Mix flour, salt, pepper and sage. Rub the mixture thoroughly into the meat, making sure it is well floured. Place meat into a roast pan, adding lemon juice and water. (If using bacon strips, cover meat entirely). Bake at 325°F until tender.

"Twin boys, Flint and Sapling, were born to the Earth Mother. Sapling was the spirit of good, who made all good things and caused corn, tobacco and fruit to grow. Flint was the spirit of evil who caused weeds and all the vermin to appear on the earth."

—*Iroquois myth*

FRIED MUSKRAT

1/4 cup flour
1/2 tsp. salt
1/4 tsp. pepper
1/2 tsp. poultry seasoning
1/4 tsp. sage

2 muskrat, cut into service-size
  pieces
Bacon fat, butter or margarine
1/2 cup water
2 tbsp. finely chopped celery
2 tbsp. finely chopped onion

Mix flour, salt, pepper, poultry seasoning and sage. Rub thoroughly into muskrat pieces, making sure pieces are thoroughly coated. Fry in bacon fat, butter or margarine. Add the 1/2 cup of water to frying pan and cook slowly for about 5 minutes. Add celery and onions. Stir and cook for 1/2 hour or until done.

MUSKRAT HASH

3 muskrats
2 large onions, diced
1 tsp. poultry seasoning
1 tsp. sage
1 tsp. garlic salt

2 tsp. salt
1 tsp. pepper
1 cup barbecue sauce
1/4 cup melted margarine

Boil muskrat until well cooked, approximately 2 1/2 hours. Drain. Rinse and remove bones. Combine onions, spices and barbecue sauce with meat. Place meat mixture into a lightly greased casserole dish. Pour melted margarine over the top. Cover and bake at 300°F for 1 hour.

MUSKRAT LOAF

2 lbs. muskrat meat, cooked,
  chopped, bones removed
1 medium onion, chopped fine
2 eggs, slightly beaten
1/2 cup bread crumbs
1 cup milk

1/2 cup catsup
2 tbsp. melted margarine
1 1/2 tsp. salt
1/2 tsp. pepper
1/4 tsp. thyme
1/4 tsp. sage

Place muskrat in a large bowl and mix in remaining ingredients. Pack lightly into a greased loaf pan and roast in a 350°F oven for 30 to 35 minutes.

PORCUPINE

The porcupine is recognized by its heavy dark brown or blackish body and a heavy short tail. The hair on a porcupine hides the quills unless the creature is alarmed.

The porcupine usually weighs 8 - 15 lbs. and is known to be very clumsy and slow moving. Its diet consists of most plants, nuts and tree bark.

Although the porcupine is well protected, it does have its enemies. Usually the porcupine wins, but on occasion, an animal learns to flip the porcupine and is able to attack the defenseless belly. Contrary to what many believe, the porcupine does not shoot its quills.

BARBECUED PORCUPINE

1/2 porcupine to each serving   Water
Vinegar   Barbecue sauce

Soak meat overnight in vinegar and water. Discard liquid. Roast on broiler pan (rack at center of oven) at 350°F for 1 hour. Spread barbecue sauce over meat and cook for 10 minutes. Turn meat over and spread barbecue sauce on meat and cook for an additional 10 minutes.

APPLE-ROASTED PORCUPINE

1 porcupine, dressed   2 tbsp. sugar
3 apples, unpeeled, quartered   4 cups water
   and seeds removed   Salt and pepper to taste

Parboil porcupine for 1 hour in salted water to cover. Drain and rinse. Place meat in a roast pan. Add apples and sprinkle the apples with the sugar. Add the water. Sprinkle meat with salt and pepper. Cover and roast 30 to 40 minutes at 375°F.

RACCOON

The raccoon is a nocturnal animal with good vision and hearing. The naked soles of its feet are extremely sensitive to touch, and the coat of the racoon ranges from black to tawny, pale grey and blonde. Raccoons have prominent black rings on their tails, and their nickname, "Bandit," bespeaks the famous black facial mask over their cheeks, eyes and nose. The average raccoon weighs about 17 lbs.

Raccoons prefer forested areas near water, river valleys and farmland. They usually live in hollow trees, logs, caves, mines and other animal burrows.

Raccoons are omnivorous, eating young birds, small mammals, carrion, poultry, fish, frogs, eggs, fruit, nuts, berries, grain and corn.

Although raccoons do not hibernate, they are inactive and stay in their dens when the temperature is below 26°F.

Raccoons are also considered an excellent table meat.

OLD-FASHIONED COOKED RACCOON

1 raccoon, dressed
Water to cover
1 tbsp. salt
1 tsp. baking soda

2 cups water
Sage
Salt and pepper to taste

Cut raccoon into serving pieces; cover with water to which the 1 tablespoon salt and the baking powder have been added. Soak overnight. Drain and rinse. Place meat pieces in a baking dish and add the 2 cups of water. Sprinkle with sage, salt and pepper. Cover with aluminum foil and bake at 375°F until tender.

One of the first things a Cherokee boy would learn is the use of the blowgun. Made of hollowed out cane, the blowguns were up to ten feet long and fired darts capable of killing small game, such as squirrels or rabbits, from as far as 60 feet away.

RACCOON ROAST

1 raccoon, dressed
2 celery stalks, chopped
3 onions, sliced thin

2 chicken bouillon cubes
Salt and pepper to taste
1 cup water

In a large pot, parboil meat for about 45 minutes in salt water (1 tablespoon of salt per quart). This helps tenderize the meat. Rinse well.

Transfer raccoon to roasting pan. Add celery, onions, bouillon cubes, salt and pepper. Add water. Cover and bake at 325°F about 1 1/2 to 2 hours or until tender.

RACCOON AND DRESSING

1 raccoon, dressed
2 cups mashed potatoes
1 onion, chopped
2 cups bread crumbs
1/2 tsp. salt

1 tsp. sage
1/2 tsp. poultry seasoning
Pepper to taste
1/4 cup bacon drippings

Parboil raccoon in salted water for about 45 minutes. Drain and rinse. Cut into service-size pieces. Combine remaining ingredients in a large bowl. Add a little water if too dry. Place raccoon pieces on half of a shallow baking dish. Dot with margarine and sprinkle with salt and pepper. Spread the dressing on the remaining half of the baking dish. Cover with aluminum foil. Bake at 350°F for 60 to 90 minutes.

RACCOON DELIGHT

Salt and pepper
1 raccoon, dressed
2 cups cut-up vegetables
2 sweet potatoes, peeled and
   diced

1 large onion, chopped
1 large apple, peeled and diced
1 can (28 oz.) sauerkraut
Few drops Tabasco sauce

Salt and pepper the entire carcass. Combine vegetables, potatoes, onion and apple. Stuff cavity of the raccoon. Place in a roasting pan stomach side up. Drain sauerkraut, reserving the juice, and spread sauerkraut over the vegetables in cavity. Mix a few drops of Tabasco sauce with reserved juice and pour over the raccoon. Cover and roast at 350°F for 3 to 4 hours or until very tender.

SQUIRREL

Squirrels today are a more common sight in the cities and towns than they are in their natural woodland habitat. Nuts and seeds are the mainstay of the squirrel's diet. These animals are busy gatherers, and store their finds for winter use.

Squirrels are found in almost all of the temperate zones. They are grey to black in color, with long busy tails, and weigh only 1 - 1 1/2 lbs.

The meat of the squirrel is considered by many to be a delectable dish.

BROILED SQUIRREL

2 squirrels
1 tsp. salt
Dash of pepper

1/4 cup melted butter for
    basting

Skin and clean squirrels. Wash thoroughly and pat dry. Cut in half lengthwise and rub with salt and pepper. Place halves on broiling rack and brush with fat. Broil 5 inches from source of heat, 20 minutes on each side. Baste every few minutes with melted butter and drippings.

SQUIRREL FRICASSEE

1 squirrel
1/2 tsp. salt
Dash of pepper
1/2 cup flour

4 slices bacon
1 tbsp. diced onion
1 1/2 tsp. lemon juice
1/3 cup broth

Skin and clean squirrel, being sure to remove scent glands from forelegs. Wash thoroughly and cut squirrel into serving pieces. Rub pieces with salt and pepper, then dredge with flour. Cut up bacon and cook over low heat until crisp. Add the squirrel and panfry with the bacon for 20 minutes, until nicely browned. Add onion, lemon juice and broth. Cover tightly and simmer for 2 hours.

SNAPPING TURTLE

The snapping turtle is a reptile having a large head with a strongly hooked beak. An exceedingly rough shell and very long tail make it easy for them to protect themselves by hiding within their shell. Snapping turtles are brown in color and range in size from 8 to 20 inches in length.

Snapping turtles are found in most bodies of fresh water. Their diet includes aquatic invertebrates, fish, reptiles, birds, mammals, carrion and vegetation. Underwater, they are inoffensive, but on land they will strike out. The snapping turtle is found from Canada in the north, south to Mexico and west to the Rockies. The meat is considered a delicacy by many. Properly prepared, it is succulent and has a unique taste.

TURTLE WITH MUSHROOMS

2 cups cooked turtle meat
1 cup mushroom stems and
   pieces

2 cups white sauce (See Chapter
   7 for recipes)
1 tbsp. sherry

Combine all ingredients in a saucepan and heat slowly. Serve over toast.

TURTLE CHOWDER

1 lb. cubed turtle meat
2 tsp. salt
1 cup chopped celery
1 cup sliced carrots
1 cup sliced turnip

1 cup chopped green peppers
1 medium onion, chopped
1 cup peas
1/2 cup milk
2 tbsp. flour or cornstarch

Boil meat in salted water until done, about 1 hour. Then add all vegetables and cook over medium heat until tender. Remove from heat and add milk. Thicken with flour or cornstarch.

TURTLE RAGOUT

1 onion, chopped
2 tbsp. butter or margarine
1 tbsp. flour
2 lbs. turtle meat, diced

1 cup water
1/4 cup sherry
1 clove garlic, minced

Saute onion in butter or margarine until tender. Blend in flour. Add remaining ingredients and simmer for 30 minutes.

TURTLE SOUP

1 lb. turtle meat, cubed
4 potatoes, quartered
4 carrots, quartered
1 onion, diced
1 cup diced turnip

1 cup chopped celery
1 cup peas
1 cup milk
Flour to thicken
1 tbsp. sugar (optional)

Boil meat until nearly tender. Add oil vegetables and simmer covered, for 1 hour. Add milk and thicken with flour. Mix in sugar, if desired.

WILD OMELETTE

6 eggs
1/4 cup milk
1/2 cup chopped onions
Salt and pepper

1 tbsp. fat
1/2 cup chopped leftover turtle
  or other wild meat
Grated cheese

Combine eggs, milk, onions, and salt and pepper. Heat fat in a skillet. Add egg mixture. Lift with a spatula allowing liquid to run underneath. Spread chopped meat and cheese over the eggs, then fold. When the cheese has melted, serve with toast.

The False Face Society of the Iroquois donned elaborate masks and turtle-shell rattles for their healing ceremonies. They were considered so powerful that the healing took only a few minutes. The cured patient automatically became a member, who could be called on to heal others.

BULLFROG

The bullfrog is the largest frog, measuring 3 1/2 to 6 inches long. It is a plain or nearly green color with a netlike pattern of gray or brown on a green background. It has a whitish underbelly, often mottled with gray, and a yellowish throat underneath. It has long hind legs, and is narrow waisted and smooth skinned.

Bullfrogs are aquatic amphibians living in lakes, ponds, bogs or sluggish portions of streams.

The legs of the bullfrog are considered a delicacy throughout many parts of North America as well as Europe.

FROG LEGS

The hind legs of the frog are the only part that can be eaten. Cut legs from body, wash in cold water, turn skin down and strip off. Cover with cold water, drain, dry and use as desired.

FRIED FROG LEGS

Prepare frog legs as above. Season with salt and pepper, dip into fine cracker crumbs, then into slightly beaten egg and again into crumbs. Let stand for 15 to 20 minutes. Fry in hot fat, until browned.

SAUTEED FROG LEGS

Prepare frog legs as above and brown in skillet in a small amount of hot fat.

BREADED FROG LEGS

1/2 tsp. salt
1/4 tsp. pepper
Flour for dredging
6 - 7 pairs frog legs, cleaned

1 tbsp. grated onion
Small amount of butter for frying
1 tsp. lemon juice

Mix salt and pepper with enough flour to dredge the frog legs. Saute onion in butter. Add dredged frog legs and lemon juice. Cook, covered, over low heat (or low flame) for 10 to 15 minutes, until legs are brown and tender.

DEEP-FRIED FROG LEGS

25 frog legs
1 cup flour
1/2 tsp. salt

1/4 tsp. pepper
3 eggs, beaten
2 1/2 cups bread crumbs

Wash and dry frog legs. In a paper bag put flour, salt and pepper. Add legs to bag and shake; then dip into beaten eggs. Roll in bread crumbs and deep-fry.

CREAM-SAUCED FROG LEGS

2 lbs. frog legs
1/3 cup flour
1 1/2 tsp. salt
1/2 tsp. dried tarragon
1/4 tsp. pepper

1/4 cup butter or margarine
2 tbsp. finely chopped onion
1 1/2 cups light cream
2 tbsp. chopped parsley

Separate frog legs into individual legs. In bag, combine flour, salt, tarragon and pepper. Shake frog legs in flour mixture a few at a time to coat thoroughly. Reserve 1 tablespoon of flour mixture.

In a large skillet brown frog legs in butter. Cook, covered, until tender, about 25 minutes. Remove legs, and keep warm.

In same skillet cook onions until tender, but not brown. Blend in reserved flour mixture. Stir in light cream; cook and stir until thickened. Spoon over frog legs. Garnish with parsley.

BATTER-FRIED FROG LEGS

1 egg, beaten
1/2 cup cornmeal
1/2 tsp. salt

1/8 tsp. pepper
2 lbs. frog legs
1/2 cup oil

Mix egg, cornmeal, salt and pepper to form a batter. Dip frog legs in batter; fry in oil in heavy skillet for 25 minutes, turning so they brown evenly on all sides.

* CHAPTER THREE *
GAME BIRDS

The age of a game bird is an important consideration in selecting the recipe to be used. The older the bird, the longer it must be cooked. Older birds are usually used in soups and stews.

A young pheasant has a pliable spur. The breastbone of a young partridge will break easily, and the leg will be plump near the foot.

The claws of a young bird are sharp; those of an old one are blunt.

If stuffing the bird before cooking, always use a cool stuffing, because bacteria will start working and render your bird unpalatable, if not unsafe to eat.

DUCKS

Ducks can generally divided into two groups: those that take their food on or from the surface of the water (*puddle ducks*) and those that take their food from under the surface (*diving ducks*). Puddle ducks (mallards, pintails, wood ducks and black ducks for example) have broad, flat bills with a turned-down projection at the tip. The legs are near the center of the body, making them adequate swimmers and well-balanced walkers. Diving ducks (bluebills, redheads, ruddy ducks) eat more animal food than puddle ducks, in addition to vegetable matter. The legs are near the rear of the body, making them excellent swimmers but clumsy on land.

All ducks require open water and are therefore migratory in northern North America.

Ducks are extremely common throughout the United States and Canada and provide excellent eating. Usually the surface-eating puddle ducks provide the more palatable fare.

ROAST DUCK WITH WILD RICE CASSEROLE

2 wild ducks, dressed
1 celery stalk, cut in half
2 small onions

2 cups water
2 strips bacon

Wash ducks in cold water and pat dry. Put half a stalk and one onion in each duck cavity. Place ducks in a roasting pan, breast side up. Pour in cold water and place a bacon strip over each duck. Cover and bake at 350°F until meat is tender, about 1 1/2 hours. Remove bacon strips and brown ducks. Remove ducks from pan and keep in a warm place.

WILD RICE CASSEROLE

1/4 lb. wild rice
1/2 cup diced bacon
1/4 cup sliced green onions
1/4 cup sliced mushrooms

1 tomato, peeled and chopped
1 tsp. garlic powder
salt and pepper
Parmesan Cheese

For the casserole wash rice in cold water. Drain. Put rice into a saucepan, cover with water and bring to a boil. Reduce heat and simmer for 60 minutes. Drain. Saute bacon, green onions and mushrooms for 5 minutes.

Put rice in a casserole dish and stir in tomato, garlic powder and bacon mixture. Season with salt and pepper. Sprinkle cheese over the casserole and bake for 20 minutes at 300°F. Serve with the ducks.

BLUEBERRY DUCK ROAST

1 1/2 cup blueberries
2 tbsp. white vinegar
1 tbsp. vegetable oil
2 tsp. brown sugar
1 tsp. salt

1/2 tsp. pepper
1/4 tsp. ground cloves
1/4 tsp. nutmeg
4 to 6 wild duck breasts

Combine all ingredients except duck breasts in a blender. Process to a coarse puree. Remove bones from duck breasts, leaving skin intact. Place breasts on a rack in roaster and coat each one with blueberry mixture. Bake at 375°F for 30 minutes, basting often.

DELICIOUS ROAST DUCK

3 wild ducks
3 small onions
3 tsp. soy sauce
1/2 tsp. salt

1/2 tsp. pepper
Garlic powder
1/2 cup marmalade
Brown sugar

Place ducks in roasting pan, putting one onion inside each duck along with 1 teaspoon of the soy sauce. Sprinkle salt, pepper and garlic powder over ducks. Then brush ducks with marmalade and sprinkle lightly with brown sugar. On each duck place 1 strip of bacon. Cover and place in oven at 375°F for 60 minutes or until tender.

DUCK IN DARK SAUCE

1 wild duck
1/2 cup cider vinegar
1/4 cup soy sauce

1/4 cup white sugar
2 tsp. garlic salt
1 tsp. ginger

Wash duck and pat dry and then cut in half. Lay halves in a shallow baking pan. Mix vinegar, soy sauce, sugar and seasonings together. Put over the duck and bake, covered, at 350°F for 1 hour.

WILD DUCK SOUP

Duck bones and scraps
1 large onion, quartered
3 carrots, chopped
1 stalk celery and leaves,
    chopped

1/4 tsp. thyme
1/4 tsp. parsley
1 cup wild rice, cooked
Salt and pepper

In a soup kettle combine duck scraps and bones with onion, carrots, celery, thyme, and parsley. Cover with cold water and slowly bring to a boil. Simmer for 1 hour, remove bones. Add wild rice and season to taste and simmer for 1 hour.

The feathers worn by the Sioux warriors were used to display specific feats of bravery they had performed in battle. A warrior who killed a foe would wear a feather with a red spot on it, while one who was wounded would wear a feather dyed red. In battle, the bravest warriors would seek out an enemy with many of these decorations.

DUCK FRICASSEE

2 wild ducks
1/4 cup flour
1/4 tsp. salt
1/4 tsp. pepper
1/4 cup butter
1 medium onion, minced

1 bay leaf
1 cup sliced mushrooms, fresh
    or canned
1/2 cup sliced green peppers
1 cup water

Clean and skin ducks; wash thoroughly and cut into serving portions. Dredge portions of duck in flour and season with salt and pepper. Melt butter in a heavy frying pan, add onion and bay leaf and brown pieces of duck on all sides.

Transfer pieces of duck to a greased casserole, and saute mushrooms and green peppers in remaining fat in frying pan for 3 minutes.

Add vegetables to duck in the casserole, add the water, cover and bake until tender in a 350°F oven.

DRESSED WILD DUCKS

2 wild ducks, dressed

STUFFING:

3 cups bread crumbs
1 cooking apple, diced
1 onion, chopped finely

1/2 cup raisins
3 tbsp. melted margarine
1 tsp. salt

Wash ducks thoroughly and pat dry. Combine all stuffing ingredients in a mixing bowl. Moisten with a little water. Stuff cavity of each duck. Place in a roasting pan and add 1 1/2 cups of water. Sprinkle salt and pepper on the ducks. Cover and roast at 375°F until tender.

CURRANT DUCK ROAST

2 small onions
2 wild ducks, cleaned and
   washed
4 cups bread crumbs
1 onion, chopped
3 tbsp. melted margarine

1 tsp. salt
1 tsp. pepper
1 tsp. sage
2 tsp. currant jelly
Cornstarch

Put 1 small onion in each duck cavity and parboil ducks for 1/2 hour. Remove onion. Then, combine bread crumbs, onion, margarine, and seasonings, and fill each duck cavity. Place ducks in a roasting pan and pour over two cups of water. Cover and roast, basting frequently, for 1 1/2 hours at 350°F. Remove ducks to a warm platter and add currant jelly to liquid. Mix in some cornstarch to thicken gravy.

WILD DUCK WITH ORANGE SAUCE

1/2 cup oil
2 onions, sliced thin
1/4 tsp. parsley

Salt and pepper to taste
Breasts of 4 ducks
Butter

Combine oil, onions, parsley, salt and pepper. Marinate the duck breasts in this mixture for 3 hours. Drain and saute in butter for 20 minutes. Arrange duck on a hot platter and pour orange sauce over it.

ORANGE SAUCE:

1 tbsp. cornstarch
1 cup orange juice

3 tbsp. sugar
1 tbsp. grated orange rind

Make a paste of cornstarch and a little of the orange juice in a sauce pan. Combine the rest of the orange juice and the sugar to the saucepan. Cook until sugar dissolves and sauce is clear and thick. Add orange rind and pour over the duck.

ROAST DUCK

Duck giblets
2 cups hazelnuts
4 green apples, chopped
1/2 lb. mushrooms, chopped
1 1/2 cup Tokay grapes

1 tsp. salt
1/4 tsp. pepper
A 5 1/2-lb. duck
2 cups apple cider

Cover duck giblets with water in small saucepan and simmer 1/2 hour. Drain, reserving 1/2 cup cooking water. Chop giblets. Combine with hazelnuts, apples, mushrooms, grapes, salt and pepper and the reserved giblet cooking water to make a dressing. Stuff duck and place it breast side up on a rack in a large roasting pan. Bake in 400°F oven for 1 hour, pricking the skin and basting with apple cider every 20 minutes. Reduce oven to 350°F and continue to roast 2 hours more, basting every 20 minutes.

MALLARD BAKE

2 mallard ducks, dressed
salt and pepper to taste
5 cooking apples

1 cup raisins
1 1/2 cups water
4 bacon strips

Season the ducks with salt and pepper inside and out. Quarter apples and remove cores. Place 3 of the apple quarters in the cavity of each duck along with a handful of raisins. Place ducks in a roasting pan and add the water. Place 2 strips of bacon over each duck and place remaining pieces of apple and raisins in the pan. Bake at 350°F until tender.

The canoe typically took a week to make and was fabricated entirely from trees: a cedar frame held together with spruce-root cords, birch bark for the hull and spruce gum to make it watertight. The process was supervised by a highly-skilled canoe maker who had learned the tradition from his father and would pass it on to his son.

GEESE

Geese are migratory birds traveling great distances in the spring and fall. They nest on the ground, and always near water. Species are the Canada, Brant, and Snow. Geese mate for life and keep their young with them until the following spring. The female incubates the eggs while the male stands guard. These geese feed on roots of aquatic plants, grasses and grain. They lose their flight feathers for a time after the eggs are hatched.

Among the Cree of Northern Canada, roast goose is the meat of choice at every wedding feast. Goose-hunting season is a festive time, and special cooking wigwams, or *mi-chu-wups*, are set up for the duration.

Is there anyone who hasn't heard the honking of the geese in the spring and fall or seen the familiar V of the flocks in the sky?

Goose meat is quite delectable as dinner fare.

STUFFED WILD GOOSE

1 wild goose, dressed
1/2 cup salad oil
1/4 cup flour
Salt and pepper to taste
1 tsp. tarragon

1/2 tsp. thyme
6 strips bacon
1 cup margarine, melted
1 cup chicken bouillon

DRESSING:

6 large potatoes, cooked and
    mashed
2 tbsp. melted margarine
1 large onion, chopped
2 stalks celery, chopped fine

6 slices bread, crumbled
2 eggs, beaten
1 tbsp. poultry seasoning
1 tsp. salt
1/2 tsp. pepper

Combine all ingredients for dressing and mix thoroughly. Place goose in a roasting pan and lightly pack stuffing into cavity. Sew the opening or skewer it closed. Rub bird well with the salad oil. Combine flour, salt, pepper, tarragon, and thyme. Sprinkle mixture over the bird. Lay bacon slices over the bird. Combine melted margarine and bouillon. Pour over goose.

Roast at 300°F, allowing 30 minutes per pound. Baste frequently. Remove bacon slices 10 to 15 minutes before removing bird from oven to allow breast of bird to brown.

WILD GOOSE WITH APPLE AND RAISIN STUFFING

1 (8-10 lb.) wild goose, dressed
1/2 cup lemon juice
1/ tsp. salt
1/2 tsp. pepper
1/2 cup margarine
1 onion, chopped
1 large cooking apple, chopped

1/2 cup raisins
4 cups bread crumbs
1/2 tsp. salt
1/4 tsp. pepper
1/4 cup bacon fat
8 slices bacon

Place goose in a roasting pan. Sprinkle goose inside and out with lemon juice, salt and pepper. Melt margarine in a skillet and add onion. Cook until tender. Mix in apple, raisins, bread crumbs, salt and pepper. Set aside to cool. Pack stuffing lightly into cavity of goose. Close the opening. Rub goose with the bacon fat. Place strips of bacon over goose. Cover and roast at 350°F for 30 minutes per pound. Baste frequently.

GOOSE GIBLET SOUP

1 tbsp. butter
2 onions, diced
Giblets and liver from an 8 to
    10-lb. goose chopped
1/2 cup peeled, chopped
    tomatoes

3 carrots, peeled, diced
1/2 lb. mushrooms, sliced
1 green pepper, cored, diced
1 clove garlic, minced
2 cups chicken stock
Salt and pepper to taste

Melt butter in a heavy kettle and saute onions until tender. Add giblets (reserve liver until later) and saute 10 minutes over low heat. Add remaining ingredients; cover and simmer for 2 hours. Add liver during the last 15 minutes. Serve with rice or biscuits.

ROAST GOOSE

Goose giblets
16 oz. bag poultry stuffing mix
2 cups cranberries, mashed
1/4 lb. mushrooms, sliced
1 lb. stewed prunes, mashed

1 tsp. salt
1/4 tsp. pepper
A 10 to 11 lb. goose
2 cups apple cider

Simmer goose giblets in salted water for 30 minutes or until tender, chop. For stuffing, mix prepared stuffing mix, cranberries, mushrooms, mashed prunes, reserved giblets, and seasonings.

Stuff goose and place breast side up on a rack in a large roasting pan and roast in a 350°F oven for 4 1/2 hours.

Prick the skin from time to time and baste every 15 minutes with cider and drippings.

"What kind of a thing is it that you are roasting?" Sapling's grandmother asked. He replied, "It is corn. My father gave it to me. And it is this that the man-beings who will dwell here on the earth will continue to eat."

—Onondaga myth

TURKEY

Many recipes for domestic turkey adapt well to wild turkey meat. Keep in mind that wild turkey has less fat and will dry out quicker. Baste often. Draping bacon strips over the bird will help.

TURKEY WITH OYSTER STUFFING

An 8-lb. turkey, with giblets
1 1/2 cups water

1 cup softened butter

STUFFING:

8 cups crumbled cornbread
10 mushrooms, chopped
18 oysters, chopped
Cooked chopped turkey giblets
2 scallions, sliced
1 cup pecans, chopped
1 clove garlic, minced

2 tbsp. chopped parsley
1/2 cup reserved giblet water
1 egg, beaten
1/4 cup melted butter
1 tsp. salt
1/4 tsp. pepper
1/2 tsp. savory

Simmer giblets in the water for 20 to 30 minutes. Drain, reserving 1/2 cup cooking water for stuffing. Cool and chop.

Mix stuffing ingredients together and stuff into body cavities, skewer cavities shut and place turkey breast side down on baking rack in large roasting pan. Rub turkey with 1/4 cup of the softened butter. Roast turkey uncovered at 325°F for 1 1/2 hours, basting every 20 minutes with remaining butter and drippings. Turn turkey so breast side is up and continue basting and baking until leg joint moves easily (30 minutes per pound).

OPEN-FIRE WILD TURKEY

1 turkey, dressed
Barbecue salt

Seasonings to taste

Wash turkey well; pat dry inside and out. Rub barbecue salt liberally on inside of turkey. Run stick diagonally through turkey from front of tail to breastbone. Tie tightly to stick.

Roast over low fire 3 - 4 hours turning every so often. Near end of roasting period, throw seasonings on fire below to burn for additional flavor.

TURKEYWILD RICE SOUP

Leftover turkey carcass and meat
9 cups water
1/4 cup chopped onion
2 small carrots, chopped
1 bay leaf

Pinch of parsley
Salt and pepper to taste
1/2 tsp. thyme
4 cups cooked wild rice

Break apart carcass. Place in pot with water, bring to boil, add remaining ingredients (except for wild rice). Reduce heat and simmer for approximately 2 hours.

Remove carcass, stripping off any remaining meat to put back into soup. Skim off any excess fat. Add wild rice. Simmer for an additional 20 minutes. Any leftover soup may be frozen.

WOODLANDS WILD TURKEY

1 turkey, dressed
Salt and pepper
1/3 cup margarine or butter
3 tbsp. flour
1/4 tsp. pepper

3 apples, sliced
1/2 cup chopped celery
1/2 cup cooking oil
Juice of 1 lemon

Prepare bird by thoroughly cleaning inside and out with cold water. Lightly rub salt and pepper on inside of turkey.

Mix margarine, flour and pepper and additional seasonings (optional) into a paste and spread all over outside of turkey. Stuff turkey with apple slices and celery pieces mixed together. Tie turkey up.

Baste turkey with oil and lemon mixture. Roast approximately 2 hours for birds under 10 pounds, 2 1/2 hours for larger birds. Baste often with oil and lemon mixture and pan juices.

STUFFED GAME HEN

6 game hens
Salt and pepper
1 cup wild rice
2 1/2 cups water
1 tsp. salt
6 tbsp. butter

4 strips bacon, diced
5 scallions, sliced
1/2 lb. mushrooms, coarsely
  chopped
1 cup hazelnuts, chopped
1 tbsp. butter

Season hens with salt and pepper. Wash wild rice, add water and salt and bring to a boil, reduce heat, simmer until water is absorbed. Melt the 6 tablespoons of butter in a skillet. In it, brown bacon and saute scallions and mushrooms. Combine with wild rice and hazelnuts.

Rub hens with the 1 tablespoon butter; stuff with stuffing. Roast at 350°F for 2 to 2 1/2 hours, basting frequently with butter and drippings.

"The bark canoe of the Chippeways is, perhaps, the most beautiful and light model of all the water crafts ever invented.... Ingeniously shaped and sewed together ... they ride upon the water, as light as a cork."
—*comment by explorer and artist, George Catlin, 1834*

PARTRIDGE

Partridge are land birds with small heads and bills, and long legs. They are brown in color and have a ruff around the neck and a fan-shaped tail. These birds are chicken-like and nest on the ground.

They are nonmigratory, although they tend to wander irregularly in winter. They are found throughout the northern hemisphere and can survive the winter months because of their ability to feed in trees. This family of birds are superb dinner fare.

Typically, these birds weigh around one pound, dressed weight.

BAKED PARTRIDGE

4 partridge, dressed
1/3 cup butter
1 small onion, halved
1 small clove garlic, chopped

1/2 cup water
1 tbsp. chopped celery
1 tsp. salt
1/4 tsp. pepper

Cut up partridge, using the breasts and thighs. Brown lightly in butter with onion and garlic. Place in small roasting pan and add water and chopped celery. Sprinkle with salt and pepper. Bake, covered, at 350°F for 1 1/2 hours. Baste frequently to prevent dryness.

PARTRIDGE WITH GRAPE JUICE

1/2 cup bacon fat
4 partridge, dressed
1 pint grape juice
1 whole clove

1 bay leaf
Cornstarch
Water

Heat bacon fat in skillet and lightly brown the partridge. Add grape juice, clove and bay leaf. Cover and simmer for 50 minutes. Remove meat to a hot platter. Discard bay leaf and clove and thicken liquid with cornstarch and water. Pour sauce over partridge and serve.

LEMON-FLAVORED PARTRIDGE

4 partridge, cut into pieces
Salt and pepper to toast
1/4 cup lemon juice
1/3 cup oil

1 clove garlic, minced
1 tsp. parsley flakes
2 tsp. oregano

Sprinkle partridge pieces with salt and pepper. In a bowl, mix lemon juice, oil, garlic, parsley and oregano. Dip each piece of meat in mixture and place on a broiler pan. Broil 15 to 20 minutes on each side. Baste occasionally with lemon-oil mixture.

PARTRIDGE CASSEROLE

1/4 cup flour
1 tsp. salt
1/4 tsp. pepper
2 partridge, cut into serving
    pieces

5 tbsp. butter or margarine
1 cup canned mushroom soup
1 1/2 cups boiling water
1 onion, sliced

Mix flour, salt, and pepper. Dredge partridge in flour until well coated. Melt butter in heavy frying pan and brown partridge on all sides. When browned, remove from pan and put pieces into well-buttered casserole dish. Pour over them mushroom soup that has been mixed with boiling water. Add onion. Bake at 350°F for 1 1/2 hours.

PARTRIDGE WITH WILD RICE DRESSING

3/4 lb. sweet sausage
1/2 cup uncooked wild rice
2 slices white bread
1/2 cup milk
1/4 cup olive oil
7 tbsp. butter
1 oz. salt pork, diced
1/2 cup water
1 large onion, diced

2 eggs, beaten
1 clove garlic, minced
2 partridge
3 thin slices salt pork
1/4 tsp. salt
1/4 tsp. pepper
1/4 cup chicken stock (or boiled
  giblet broth)

To prepare dressing, remove casing from sausage and cut into small pieces. Soak rice in warm water for 15 minutes and then drain. Cook in salted water for 20 minutes and drain again. Soak bread in milk; drain, squeeze and shred. In a skillet, heat 3 tablespoons of the oil, 4 tablespoons of the butter and add salt pork and onions. Cook until golden brown. Then add sausage and cook 20 minutes. Add the water to skillet, cover and cook for 3 minutes. Remove from heat and let cool. Then add to skillet shredded bread, beaten eggs, rice and garlic. Mix well and use to stuff birds.

Oil roasting pan with remaining olive oil and butter. Place birds breast down. Cover with salt pork slices, sprinkle with salt and pepper, and pour stock over. Roast at 450°F for 10 minutes and then turn down to 300°F and roast for 1 hour.

PARTRIDGE STEW

2 partridge, cut into serving
  pieces
1/4 cup butter
1 onion, finely chopped
1 carrot, thinly sliced
1 tsp. chopped parsley
1 tsp. poultry seasoning

3 tbsp. flour
1 can chicken and rice soup
1/4 cup water
1 small can mushroom pieces
  and stems
Salt and pepper to taste

Brown partridge pieces in butter in a large saucepan. Add onion, carrot, parsley and poultry seasoning. Cook slowly. Stir in flour, gradually adding soup, water and mushrooms. Season with salt and pepper. Simmer, covered, until tender.

PARTRIDGE WITH BREAD SAUCE

4 partridge breasts   1/2 cup water
4 strips bacon

Wrap each breast in a strip of bacon and place in a small roasting pan. Add the water, cover and roast for 30 minutes at 350°F. Serve with Bread Sauce.

BREAD SAUCE:

2 cups milk   1/2 tsp. salt
1 small onion, diced   Dash of nutmeg
1 cup light bread crumbs   1 tbsp. butter

Pour milk in a saucepan. Add onions and bring to a boil. Add bread crumbs, salt, nutmeg and butter; reduce heat, stir and simmer for 15 minutes. Pour over partridge before serving.

PARTRIDGE PIE

1 cup cooked cubed partridge   1 cup well seasoned gravy
3/4 cup peas   Biscuit dough
1/2 cup cooked carrots

Combine partridge, vegetables and gravy in a casserole dish. Top with biscuit dough. Bake at 450°F for 15 to 20 minutes.

PHEASANT AND QUAIL

These birds are chicken-like and they take their food from the ground. They suffer in winter because of their inability to feed above the snow cover. Both pheasant and quail are noted for their beautiful appearance.

Members of this family include the Bobwhite, California, Mountain and Gambel's Quail. Ring-necked pheasants are very tasty if you are fortunate enough to bag one. Ring-necks typically dress out at 1 1/2 to 2 1/2 pounds; quail at 5 to 7 ounces.

CREAM-ROASTED PHEASANT

Pheasant, dressed
Flour
Salt and pepper

Butter
Cream

Cut pheasant into serving pieces. Wash and pat dry. Dredge with flour, salt and pepper. Fry in butter until light-brown on both sides. Place in a roasting pan and add enough cream to cover the pieces. Bake at 350°F until tender, about 20 minutes per pound.

ROAST WILD PHEASANT

1 pheasant, dressed
Lemon juice
1 cup chopped celery
1 cup chopped onion

1/2 cup water
1 cup melted margarine
Salt and pepper to taste
1/2 cup grape jelly

Wash meat and pat dry. Wipe cavity well with lemon juice. Combine celery and onion. Stuff pheasant with mixture but do not close cavity. Fold wings over the back, tuck in the neck skin and hold with a skewer; tie legs together. Place breast side up on a rack in a roasting pan. Add the water and the melted margarine, sprinkle with salt and pepper, cover with foil and roast at 350°F until tender. Allow 25 to 20 minutes per pound. When meat is cooked, remove foil and add 1/2 cup grape jelly to drippings. Cook uncovered for 15 minutes, basting frequently.

Pheasant

Quail

ROAST PHEASANT

2 pheasants
3/4 cup butter
1/2 tsp. thyme
2 tsp. salt

18 juniper berries
1/8 tsp. pepper
2 lbs. seedless grapes
1 cup broken nut meats

Melt butter and stir in seasoning and crushed juniper berries. Rub birds inside and out with butter mixture. Mash half the grapes, mix in rest of grapes and remaining ingredients. Stuff birds and truss. Place birds on rack in baking pan and bake at 425° F for 15 minutes. Reduce heat to 350°F and roast 45 minutes more basting every 10 minutes with drippings.

QUAIL AND PEPPERS

1/2 cup oil
1/2 cup chopped onion
4 quail, quartered
1/2 tsp. salt

1/8 tsp. cayenne
1 cup tomatoes
2 sweet red peppers, sliced thin
2 green peppers, sliced thin

Heat oil in large Dutch oven. Add onion and saute until brown. Add quail and cook on both sides until brown. Sprinkle salt and cayenne over quail pieces. Add tomatoes and cook, covered, for 30 minutes on low heat. Add red and green peppers. Cook for an additional 20 minutes or until peppers are tender.

PHEASANT WITH WILD RICE STUFFING

1 pheasant, dressed
Lemon juice
1 1/2 cups wild rice
3 cups boiling water
1 tsp. salt
1/4 cup margarine
1 tbsp. bacon fat

2 cups mushrooms, stems and
  pieces
1/2 cup chopped onion
1/4 cup chopped celery
1/2 cup stewed tomatoes
1 tbsp. poultry seasoning

Wash meat and pat dry. Rub cavity well with lemon juice. Wash rice in cold water, drain, then place rice in a saucepan. Cover with the boiling water; add salt and simmer for 55 to 60 minutes. Add more water when necessary. When rice is tender, drain.

In a skillet over low heat, melt margarine and bacon fat. Saute mushrooms, onions and celery until tender. In a mixing bowl place tomatoes and seasonings. Mix in rice and mushroom mixture. Stuff bird, then place on a rack in a roasting pan. Pour over 2 cups of water. Cover bird loosely with aluminum foil and bake at 350°F until tender.

BRAISED QUAIL

6 tbsp. butter
4 quail

1/4 cup cider

Place 1 tablespoon of the butter in the cavity of each quail and close opening with skewer. Melt remaining 2 tablespoons of butter in heavy skillet and brown the birds over low heat. Place in casserole dish. Add cider and cover and bake for 20 minutes or until the birds are tender.

PIGEONS AND DOVES

This family of birds is noted for their small heads, small bills and short legs. They are extremely fast flying birds, with pointed wings. They feed on the ground on weed seeds and waste grain. Pigeons and doves are prolific and are found in almost all areas of North American and Mexico. They are prized table meat. Average dressed weight per bird is 4 to 6 ounces.

DOVE CASSEROLE

4 or 5 doves, dressed
1 carrot, grated
1 celery stalk, chopped
1 can cream of chicken soup
1/2 cup condensed milk

2 tbsp. fat, melted
1 cup peas
1/4 tsp. rosemary
Salt and pepper to taste

Place doves in a casserole dish. Sprinkle carrot and celery over doves. Mix together remaining ingredients and pour over doves. Cover and bake at 375°F for about 2 hours.

The Wren is the messenger of the birds and announces births to the rest of the birds. When a boy is born, the Wren will sing, "The whistle of an arrow! My shins will burn," because she knows that when the boy grows older he will hunt the birds with a blowgun and roast them in the fire.

—*Cherokee*

DOVES WITH MUSHROOM SAUCE

8 to 10 doves, dressed
Flour
1/4 cup butter
1 onion, sliced
1 can mushroom gravy
1 can (10 oz.) whole
   mushrooms
1/4 cup dry red wine (optional)
1/2 tsp. sage
Salt and pepper to taste

Dredge the doves in flour. Melt butter in a heavy skillet and sear the doves. Add onions and saute until soft. Combine remaining ingredients; mix thoroughly. Pour over doves and add enough water to cover doves completely. Cover skillet and cook over low heat for 1 to 1 1/2 hours.

PIGEON PIE

5 pigeons, cleaned and washed
1/2 lb. salt pork, diced
2 tsp. salt
Half an onion, minced
1 stalk celery, chopped
3 whole cloves
Cornstarch
Pastry for double-crust pie
Potato, thinly sliced

Cut pigeons in half and place in a large cooking pot along with the salt pork. Cover with water and bring to a boil. Skim surface. Add salt, onion, celery and cloves and simmer for 20 minutes. Take out the meat and thicken the liquid with cornstarch

Remove bones from the pigeon and cut larger pieces of meat into small chunks. Line baking dish with pastry and cover bottom with thinly sliced raw potatoes. Add the meat pieces and cover with another layer of thinly sliced potatoes. Pour in liquid and then cover with pastry. Make two slits in center of pie to allow steam to escape. Bake for 30 minutes at 350°F.

PIGEONS WITH SAUSAGE STUFFING

6 pigeons, dressed
Salt
1 lb. sausage meat
2 onions, chopped
1 cup mashed potatoes
1/2 tsp. sage

Salt and pepper
6 tbsp. butter, melted
6 slices bacon
1 1/2 cups chicken stock
1/2 cup white wine

Rub pigeons with salt inside and out. In a skillet, brown the sausage meat over low heat. Pour off fat and add onions, and saute until soft. Stir in mashed potatoes and season with sage, salt and pepper. Stuff mixture into the birds cavities and truss. Place birds, breast side up, on rack in a roasting pan and brush with melted butter. Cut each bacon slice in half and attach to breasts by securing with toothpicks. Roast 20 minutes, basting and turning birds twice. Remove the bacon and roast 20 minutes longer, until breasts are brown and the birds are tender. Place birds on a hot platter and keep warm. Pour the fat from the roasting pan and add the stock and wine and bring to a boil. Simmer until volume is reduced to half. Serve sauce in gravy boat.

✳ CHAPTER FOUR ✳
FISH AND SEAFOOD

Catching fish with a hook and line, as in modern sport-fishing, was not the preferred method of most tribes due to its relative inefficiency.

Fish were harvested in a number of different ways, most of which are considered unsportsmanlike or are even illegal now. Elaborate traps, built of saplings and interwoven with twigs, were built at strategic places in the mouths of rivers and low-tide areas. Other tribes netted fish with nets made of hand-worked natural fibers. Bow-hunting and spearing of fish were common among almost all tribes. Certain tribes developed herbal-based poisons which, when introduced into a lake or small stream, stunned fish and caused them to float helplessly to the surface, where they could be gathered easily. Night-fishing, using fish oil lanterns for illumination, was also practiced by native people.

Fish should be cleaned (see chapter 5) immediately after catching and stored in a cold place until ready to use or frozen if they are not going to be eaten the same day.

If fish has cooked sufficiently, the meat should flake at the touch of a fork.

BASS

The bass in an abundant fish. It can be found in sluggish or clear water depending on the variety. The color is dark green on the back, dull greenish-silver on the sides and pale below. Weight of a bass is about 2-3 lbs. Bass are found in the Great Lakes region.

CARP

Carp is a large, coarse fish with a saw-edged spine on the dorsal and anal fin. It has 2 pairs of barbels at the mouth. It is a dusky greenish or brownish on the back and side; yellowish on the lower sides and belly and reddish on the fins. It reaches a length of 2 ft. or more and a weight of more than 7 lbs.

CATFISH

The catfish has a boney ridge from head to dorsal fin. It has 4 barbels around its mouth. Its color varies from dark yellowish brown to black. It reaches a length of 12-18 inches and seldom weighs more than 1 or 2 pounds. It is found in the Great Lakes region, and is very good to eat.

EEL

The eel has a long snake-like form with a large mouth, projecting lower jaw, and will develop pectoral fins. The scales are small and imbedded. It is variable in color; running from brown to yellowish-olive with a paler underside. It may reach lengths of 4-5 ft. and weigh only 7 lbs.

MUSKIE (MUSKELLUNGE)

Muskie has a long pointed head, formidable teeth and fine scales. The dorsal and anal fins are located opposite one another, near the tail. They are usually dark gray on the back, grayish-silver with round or squarish blackfish spots on their sides and a white belly. The length is 4 ft. and weighs 50 lbs. They are found in the Great Lakes region.

PICKEREL

The pickerel has a perch-like structure with 2 dorsal fins, a longish pike-like head and many sharp canine teeth. The scales are small and rough. Color varies but is usually a mottled dark olive and brassy. The belly is yellowish or white. Medium-size fish reach lengths under 3 ft. and weigh less than 20 lbs. They are also found in the Great Lakes region.

PIKE

Similar in features to the muskellunge, the pike is usually under 4 ft. and under 40 lbs. It has a long pointed head, formidable teeth and fine scales. The dorsal and anal fins are located near the tail, opposite one another. They are usually dark gray on the back, grayish-silver with roundish or square spots on the sides and white on the belly. They are found in northern North America.

SALMON

Salmon vary in size from 15 to 100 lbs. They are found in the Atlantic and Pacific Oceans, rivers that flow into them, and the Great Lakes and their tributaries. They are delicious to eat.

SMELT

Smelt are small, slender fish. They have a translucent greenish back with silvery sides. They rarely exceed 10 inches in length. They are found from Virginia northward to the Gulf of the St. Lawrence.

LARGE LAKE TROUT

A large lake trout has a very dark to pale gray back and sometimes has greenish sides. It is profusely spotted. It can grown to a very large size, weighing up to 80 lbs. It is found in deepwater lakes from the Great Lakes north to Labrador, Hudson Bay and Alaska.

WHITEFISH

The whitefish have a small mouth with distinct lower jaw. They have long slender gill-rakers. They are a deep bodied and compressed fish. The fish is olive green with white sides. The fish varies in size, the longest being over 2 ft. and weighing 23 lbs. It has soft flesh, therefore it spoils rapidly but is an excellent table fish. It is found in the Great Lakes region, northward.

FRIED SMELTS WITH HOLLANDAISE SAUCE

Smelts
Salt
1 cup flour

2 eggs, beaten
1 cup bread crumbs
Fat for frying

To clean smelt, make a cut up the stomach with a pair of sharp scissors. Remove the intestines. Wash and pat dry. Dredge the smelt with salt and flour mixture. Dip the smelt in the beaten eggs and roll in the bread crumbs. Fry in hot fat, hot enough to brown a cube of bread in 60 seconds. After putting in the fish, reduce the heat so that the fish may be sufficiently cooked without becoming too brown. Cook for 3 or 4 minutes or until nicely browned. Drain. Garnish with lemon or parsley and serve with Hollandaise Sauce.

HOLLANDAISE SAUCE

3 tbsp. butter
2 egg yolks, beaten
Dash of cayenne

1/4 tsp. salt
3 cups boiling water
1 tbsp. lemon juice

In a saucepan, cream the butter and egg yolks. Add cayenne and salt and mix in the water. Simmer until thick stirring constantly. Remove from heat and mix in the lemon juice.

*I shall go to see, I
shall go to see,
    The ears that are
ripe and ready.
    I shall go to see, I
shall go to see,
    The blossoms that
make gray the field.
    I shall go to see, I
shall go to see,
    The ears that will
cause smoke to rise
from my house.
    I shall go to see, I
shall go to see,
    The day of harvest.
        —Osage song*

TROUT WITH ALMONDS

1 fresh trout, per person
Butter
Salt and pepper
Juice of 2 lemons

1/4 cup butter
1/2 cup blanched sliced
    almonds
Parsley

Rub trout with butter and season with salt and pepper. Pour lemon juice over fish. Place in a greased baking dish and bake at 350°F until cooked through. Meanwhile melt the 1/4 cup butter in a saucepan. Add almonds and cook until brown. Pour butter and browned almonds over trout and garnish with parsley. Serve.

CORNBREAD-STUFFED TROUT

1 (3 lb.) trout, cleaned
1 cup crumbled cornbread
1 cup soft bread crumbs
1/2 cup chopped celery
1/4 cup finely chopped onion
2 tbsp. chopped green pepper

1/2 tsp. salt
1/4 tsp. sage
Pepper
1/4 cup water
3 tbsp. melted butter

Season fish generously with salt. Place in a well-greased shallow baking pan. Mix cornbread, bread crumbs, celery, onion, green pepper, the 1/2 tsp. salt, the sage and pepper to taste. Gradually add the water to the bread mixture, tossing to mix. Stuff fish loosely with mixture. Brush fish generously with melted butter and cover with foil. Bake at 350°F for 45-60 minutes.

TOASTED CHEESE FILLETS

8 trout fillets
Salt and pepper
1 cup corn meal
1 cup cooking oil

8 slices bread
8 slices velveta cheese
Salad dressing

Sprinkle fillets with salt and pepper, then coat with cornmeal. Heat cooking oil until a droplet of water bounces off it. Drop in fillets. At the same time, toast bread. When fillets are golden brown and crisp on the first side, turn over and lay a slice of cheese on the browned side. Continue frying until cheese begins to melt. Drain on a paper towel. Place each fillet on a slice of hot buttered toast and top with salad dressing.

BARBECUED STUFFED FISH

An 8-to-10 lb. trout, cleaned
Salt and pepper
Salad oil

1/2 cup butter, melted
1/4 cup lemon juice

Wash fish in cold water and pat dry. Rub cavity with salt and pepper. Stuff with Garden Vegetable Stuffing, prepared according to instructions below. Close opening with skewers. Brush fish with salad oil. Place fish into a wire basket 4-6 inches from coals. Cook for 45 minutes, turning 3 times and basting with a mixture of the butter and the lemon juice.

GARDEN VEGETABLE STUFFING

1/4 cup butter
1 cup fine chopped onion
2 cups dry bread cubes
1 cup coarsely shredded carrots
1 cup chopped mushrooms
1/2 cup parsley flakes

1 1/2 tbsp. lemon juice
1 egg, beaten
1 clove garlic, minced
2 tbsp. salt
1/4 tsp. marjoram
1/4 tsp. pepper

Melt butter. In it saute onion in butter until tender. Remove from heat and mix in remaining ingredients.

FISH CAKES

These fish cakes are nothing like the kind bought in stores. The difference in taste is like night and day.

2 cups cooked trout
3 cups mashed potatoes
1/4 cup butter
1 onion, chopped fine

Salt and pepper to taste
1 egg, well beaten
Bread crumbs

Combine all ingredients (except egg) and shape into balls. Dip balls into the beaten egg, and roll in bread crumbs. Fry in a hot skillet using just enough fat to keep cakes from burning. Turn often so they will cook evenly. Serve hot.

POACHED LAKE TROUT WITH WHITE SAUCE

3 to 4 lbs. lake trout fillets
1/2 cup milk
1/2 cup water
4 slices lemon
1/2 tsp. allspice

1/2 tsp. salt
1 sprig parsley
2 cups White Sauce
Lemon juice to taste
2 hard-boiled eggs, chopped

In a frying pan combine fish, milk, water, lemon slices, allspice, salt and parsley. Cover and cook over low heat until tender. Place on platter.

Combine hot white sauce, lemon juice and chopped eggs. Pour over fish and serve.

WHITE SAUCE:

1/4 cup butter
1/4 cup flour

2 cups milk

In a saucepan melt butter. Stir in flour until it is all absorbed. Slowly stir in the milk. Cook, stirring constantly, until thickened.

TROUT SCALLOPS

1 tbsp. butter
1 lb. cooked trout
Salt and pepper to taste
2 tbsp. water
1/2 cup milk

2 eggs
1 tsp. chopped chives
1 tsp. chopped parsley
1/2 cup bread crumbs

In a saucepan melt butter; add the cooked trout. Season with salt and pepper. Pour water over fish and simmer in saucepan with lid on for 10 minutes. Beat eggs and milk together. Stir into fish, adding chives and parsley. Pour into oven dish. Top with bread crumbs. Bake at 350°F for 15 minutes.

In the Southeast, among the Cherokee, Creek and others, the powdered seeds and bruised bark of the Horse Chestnut was thrown into ponds and pools. It would intoxicate the fish and they would rise to the surface, stunned, where the fishermen could gather them up with ease.

FISH CHEEKS

Fish cheeks from pickerel or lake trout

.1 egg, beaten

Salt and pepper to taste

6 - 8 crackers, crumbled

Bacon fat or cooking oil

The cheeks of pickerel and lake trout are large enough to use. They are boneless, skinless and considered a delicacy. Wash well. Mix egg in the salt and pepper. Dip cheeks into the egg and then roll in the crumbs. Fry over medium heat in fat or oil.

BASIC FRIED WHITEFISH

1 cup cornmeal

1 tsp. salt

1/2 tsp. pepper

3 lbs. whitefish

1/4 cup bacon fat

1/2 tsp. lemon juice

1 1/2 tsp. Worcestershire sauce

Mix cornmeal thoroughly with salt and pepper. Roll fish in the cornmeal mixture. Heat bacon fat in a heavy skillet. Brown fish 6 to 8 minutes on each side or until fish flakes easily with a fork. Mix lemon juice with Worcestershire sauce and pour over fish when serving.

WHITEFISH AND NOODLE CASSEROLE

8 ounces noodles, cooked

2 1/2 cups tomato sauce

1 medium onion, sliced

2 lbs. whitefish fillets

1/4 tsp. salt

1/4 tsp. pepper

1/4 tsp. basil

Grease casserole dish and add cooked noodles and tomato sauce. Put in sliced onions and then fish fillets. Sprinkle with salt, pepper and sweet basil. Bake at 300°F for 30 minutes or until done to taste.

JELLIED BAKED WHITEFISH

1 pkg. lemon jelly powder
1 3/4 cups hot tomato juice
1/4 tsp. Tabasco sauce
1/4 cup mild vinegar

1 cup flaked whitefish (baked)
1 1/2 cups chopped vegetables
(cooked)

Dissolve jelly powder in hot tomato juice and Tabasco sauce. Add vinegar. Chill. When slightly thickened, mix in flaked whitefish and vegetables. Chill until firm. Garnish with deviled eggs, cheese balls, pickles or olives.

BASS FRY

2 lbs. bass fillets
1 cup milk

1 cup pancake mix
Clear fat for frying

Dip fillets into milk; then dredge with pancake mix. Fry in hot fat. Drain cooked pieces on paper towels.

BASS WITH HERBS

1 bass, cleaned
1/4 cup butter
1 small clove garlic, chopped
2 onion slices, minced

1/2 tsp. chopped parsley
1 tsp. tarragon leaves, chopped
Salt and pepper to taste
2 tbsp. lemon juice

Prepare bass for pan-frying. Melt butter in a skillet. Add garlic, onion, parsley and tarragon. Saute 2 minutes. Season fish with salt and pepper; then cook gently in the herb-butter mixture until tender. Remove bass and place on a hot serving dish. Add lemon juice to sauce in skillet; heat and pour over fish.

DANDY PERCH

Butter and vegetable oil
1 bunch dandelion shoots
1 garlic clove, chopped fine

10 -12 small perch, cleaned
White wine vinegar

Using equal amounts of butter and oil, saute young dandelion shoots with garlic. Remove and set aside in a warm oven. Use the same oil to fry fish quickly, a few minutes on each side. Sprinkle wine vinegar sparingly over fish. Serve covered with dandelion shoots.

FISH CHOWDER

1/4 lb. bacon
3 onions, sliced
4 small potatoes, pared, cubed
1 tsp. salt
1 cup boiling water

1 lb. pickerel fillets
3 cups milk
1 tbsp. butter
2 tbsp. chopped parsley

Chop bacon. Fry bacon slowly in a heavy fry pan or saucepan until crisp and golden brown. Lift out bacon bits and set aside. Add onions to fat and cook until transparent. Add potatoes, salt and water. Cut fish into 2-inch squares; drop over potatoes. Cover and simmer until potatoes are tender and fish flakes, approximately 20 minutes. Add milk and heat. More salt may be added if necessary. Just before serving, drop butter, bacon and parsley into chowder; do not stir.

FISH A LA CREME

4 lbs. pickerel
Water

2 tbsp. salt

Place fish into a large saucepan; cover with salted water and bring to a boil. Reduce heat; cover and simmer for approximately 1 hour. Drain and place on a platter.

SAUCE:

3 cups milk
2 tbsp. flour
2 tbsp. lemon juice
1 small chopped onion

1 tbsp. chopped parsley
Dash of nutmeg
Salt and pepper
1 tbsp. butter

Blend milk and flour in a saucepan thoroughly. Stir in lemon juice, onion, parsley, nutmeg, salt and pepper. Place saucepan over medium heat and stir until thickened. Mix in butter. Pour over fish and serve.

MACARONI FISH PIE

3/4 cup macaroni	Water
1 lb. pickerel	1 tsp. salt

CHEESE SAUCE:

2 tbsp. butter	Dash of dry mustard
1/4 cup all-purpose flour	Salt, pepper, garlic
1 1/4 cups milk	3/4 cup grated cheddar cheese

Cook macaroni according to package directions. Meanwhile, simmer fish in a little salted water until tender. Remove fish and break into large flakes.

To prepare sauce, heat butter in a pan, then stir in flour and cook 2 - 3 minutes over low heat. Gradually add milk and seasonings. Bring to a boil and cook until thickened. Add grated cheese, but do not reboil.

Place drained macaroni and fish into a hot dish and top with cheese sauce. Place under broiler for 2 - 3 minutes, or until top is bubbly.

BAKED STUFFED PICKEREL

A 4 lb. pickerel	Melted butter
Salt and pepper	Paprika if desired

Clean and scale pickerel, leaving head and tail intact. Sprinkle inside of fish with salt and pepper. Prepare stuffing. Stuff fish and skewer the opening closed. (Note: Any extra stuffing can be cooked around the fish.) Brush all sides of fish with melted butter. Season with salt and pepper. Sprinkle with paprika, if desired. Place in a baking dish and cover with foil. Bake at 350°F for 30 - 35 minutes.

One Seminole method of fishing involved a trap made by sewing hides over a long tube of wooden hoops. They would use a plant poison of buckeye or devil's shoestring in a river pool and "herd" the stunned fish into the tube, closing the ends with drawstrings

STUFFING:

2 cups chopped spinach	1 cup brown rice, cooked
1/2 cup chopped onion	1 tbsp. Worcestershire sauce
1/2 cup grated cheese	

Mix all ingredients together.

OVEN COOKED WHITEFISH

4 whitefish fillets
1/2 cup milk
1 1/2 tsp. salt

1/2 tsp. pepper
1/2 cup cornmeal
1/3 cup cooking oil

Dip fillets in the milk mixed with salt and pepper; then coat with cornmeal. Heat half the oil in a baking pan. Arrange fillets and sprinkle with remaining oil. Bake at 475°F for 20 minutes, or until fish has browned and flakes easily. Serve with your favorite sauce.

WHITEFISH WITH EGG SAUCE

3 lbs. whitefish, cleaned
Water

2 tbsp. salt
1 tbsp. butter

Lay fish split side down in a large skillet that has a tight fitting lid. Add enough water to cover fish; then add salt and butter. Cover and simmer 45 minutes. Do not boil. Drain.

SAUCE:

2 tbsp. butter
1 tbsp. flour

1 cup milk
3 hard-boiled eggs, sliced thin

Melt butter in a saucepan and stir in flour until well blended. Slowly mix in milk and bring to a boil. Stir in eggs. Remove from heat. Pour sauce over fish and serve.

BAKED FISH

2 tbsp. oil
1/2 cup chopped onion
1/4 cup chopped celery
1/4 cup chopped green pepper
1/4 cup chopped carrots
1 small chopped tomato

1/2 cup water
1 tsp. dill seed
2 lbs. fresh fillets
1/2 tsp. salt
1/4 tsp. pepper
1 tbsp. lemon juice

In a skillet, combine oil, onion, celery, green pepper and carrot. Cook until tender. Stir in tomato and water, dill and bring to a boil. Then simmer for 10 minutes. Scatter half of this mixture in a baking dish, place fish on top and add remaining mixture. Sprinkle with salt, pepper and lemon juice. Bake at 400°F for 20 minutes.

BAKED FISH WITH CHILI SAUCE

Fish, whole or filleted
2 tbsp. chili sauce
1 tbsp. tomato sauce

1/2 cup sour cream
1 tbsp. chopped parsley

Place cleaned fish (skinned removed) in a greased casserole dish. Mix chili sauce, tomato sauce and sour cream together and pour over fish. Sprinkle with parsley. Bake covered at 350°F for 25 minutes.

FISH FILLETS

2 1/2 lb. fresh fish fillets
3 tbsp. fat, melted
2 eggs, beaten
2 tbsp. rice

1 tsp. salt
1/2 tsp. pepper
1 cup evaporated milk, chilled

Chop fillets and add melted fat, eggs, rice, salt and pepper. Whip the chilled milk stiffly and fold in. Bake at 325°F for 45 minutes in a greased 1 1/2-quart casserole dish.

OLD ENGLISH FISH

4 portions or a whole fish
Salt and pepper
3 small onions, sliced
2 apples, chopped

2 bay leaves
1 1/4 cups cider
Lemon

Season fish with salt and pepper. Place in a greased casserole dish. Add onions and apples. Top with bay leaves. Then pour cider over dish. Bake in 325°F oven until fish flakes easily. Serve with lemon.

The Seminole of Florida were not a tribe until the late 1700s. Made up of escaped slaves and bands of Creeks who fled from the settlers, the name comes from the Spanish word semonali, *meaning "runaways."*

WHOLE FISH IN FOIL

A 4-5 lb. whole fish, dressed and head removed

Tear off a sheet of extra-heavy foil long enough to wrap twice the length of the fish, plus 3 inches. Place fish in foil. Pour marinade over fish. Bring extending half of foil over fish and seal the 3 sides with double folds. Refrigerate for 1 hour.

Place fish on grill approximately 5 inches from heat. Cook for 45 to 60 minutes turning once or twice, until fish flakes easily with fork.

MARINADE:

1 clove garlic, minced
1 tsp. oregano
1 tsp. salt
1/2 tsp. basil
1/2 tsp. thyme

Dash freshly ground pepper
1/2 cup corn oil
1/4 cup lemon juice
1/4 cup chopped onion

Mix garlic, oregano, salt, basil, thyme and pepper. Stir in corn oil, lemon juice and onions.

SPECIAL FISH CHOWDER

1/2 lb. fish, fresh or frozen
1 stalk celery, chopped
1 small onion, chopped
1 medium carrot, thinly sliced
1 tbsp. margarine
Boiling water

1 tsp. salt
1/2 tsp. pepper
3/4 cup elbow macaroni
1 1/2 cups milk
1 tbsp. parsley

Cut fish into bite-sized pieces and set aside. Saute celery, onion and carrot in margarine for 5 minutes. Add boiling water, salt and pepper. Cover and simmer for 10 minutes. Add macaroni and simmer for 5 minutes. Add fish and simmer, covered, for 10 minutes longer. Stir occasionally. Add milk and heat without boiling. Garnish with parsley leaves and serve.

Thaw frozen fish in milk. The milk draws out the frozen taste and provides a fresh caught taste.

SALMON WITH AVOCADO SAUCE

3 tbsp. butter
1/2 cup chopped onion

4 salmon steaks
1 - 2 cups chicken broth

Melt butter and saute onions until translucent. Add salmon and saute 1 minute on each side. Cover with broth, bring to a gentle boil, turn heat down to low and poach 7 minutes more. Remove salmon to serving platter and keep warm. Reduce liquid to 1/2 cup and set aside for Avocado Sauce.

AVOCADO SAUCE:

2 tbsp. butter
1 1/2 tbsp. flour
1/2 cup hot milk
1/2 cup salmon broth

3 tbsp. lemon juice
1 ripe avocado, chopped
Dash Tabasco sauce
Salt and pepper to taste

Melt butter in saucepan, stir in flour and cook 2 minutes. Add milk and broth: simmer 5 minutes, stirring constantly until thickened. Pour into blender, add remaining ingredients and puree. Serve over salmon steaks.

DILLY FRIED SALMON

6 salmon
1 1/2 tsp. salt
1/4 tsp. pepper

1/2 cup butter
2 tsp. dillweed
1 tbsp. lemon juice.

Cut fish almost through lengthwise and spread open. Sprinkle with salt and pepper. Melt butter in 10-inch skillet: add dill. Place two fish flesh side down into hot dill butter: fry 2 to 3 minutes a side over moderate heat. Remove fish to a warm plate and repeat with remaining fish. When last fish is cooked, lower heat to simmer and stir in lemon juice. Pour sauce over fish.

SALMON BAKED IN KELP

3 fresh kelp fronds
2 cups kelp stems
3 medium onions, chopped
1/2 cup butter

10 cups bread crumbs
2 eggs, beaten
Salt, pepper, garlic to taste
1 large salmon

Wash kelp in fresh saltwater. Cut off the stems and chop them. Saute onions and kelp in butter until onion is translucent. Add crumbs, eggs and seasoning to make stuffing. Clean fish, pack stuffing inside it, wrap in a layer of kelp, then foil. Bury fish in hot coals and bake approximately 3 hours.

GRILLED SALMON STEAKS

30 juniper berries
6 salmon steaks

Salt and pepper to taste
Lemon wedges

Crush berries slightly, press halfway down in steaks. Grill over coals for 3 minutes on each side. Season with salt and pepper. Serve with lemon wedges.

SALMON WITH SKUNK CABBAGE

1 small onion, minced
2 tbsp. butter
Salt and pepper

1 medium salmon
1 lemon
4 skunk cabbage leaves

Saute onion in butter until translucent: add salt and pepper. Rub salmon with cut lemon and baste inside and out with butter mixture. Wrap in skunk cabbage leaves and bake over charcoal for 2 hours.

SALMON WITH WATERCRESS

1/4 cup butter
4 salmon fillets
2 cups chopped mushrooms
4 scallions, sliced thinly
1 1/2 tsp. minced garlic

1 cup cream
1/2 tsp. salt
1/4 tsp. pepper
1 bunch watercress

Melt butter in saucepan; brush melted butter on fillets and set aside. Saute mushrooms, scallions and garlic until scallions are translucent; add cream and seasonings and reduce until sauce coats a spoon. Mince watercress and add to sauce. Grill fillets 5 minutes per side. Spoon sauce over salmon and serve.

POACHED SALMON WITH MUSHROOMS

2 cups chicken broth
6 medium mushrooms, sliced
2 scallions, sliced
1 sweet red pepper, sliced

2 tsp. minced parsley
1 tsp. salt
1/4 tsp. pepper
6 salmon steaks (1 in. thick)

Simmer all ingredients (except salmon) in the chicken broth for 10 minutes. Cool to room temperature. Place salmon steaks in a large skillet, cover with broth and simmer for 15 to 20 minutes. Remove to warm plate. Boil broth down to 1 cup. Serve each steak topped with broth mixture. Salmon may be served hot or cold.

SALMON CAKES

1 lb. flaked salmon
1/3 cup cornmeal
2/3 cup milk

2 eggs, lightly beaten
10 juniper berries, crushed
Salt and pepper to taste

Mix all ingredients together, form into thin patties and fry until browned on both sides.

SMOKED SALMON WITH EGGS

6 eggs
1/8 tsp. pepper
1 tbsp. minced chives

2 tbsp. butter
1/2 lb. smoked salmon in
    julienne strips

Beat the eggs with the pepper until frothy. Stir in the chives. Melt butter in a large skillet, pour in the egg mixture and add the smoked salmon. Cook slowly, stirring, until the eggs are soft-cooked.

"I buried my father in that beautiful valley of winding waters. I love that land more than all the rest of the world."
    —*Chief Joseph, 1916 when asked about the Wallowa Valley of the Nez Perce*

FLOUNDER WITH MUSSEL SAUCE

2 doz. mussels
1/2 cup water
2 tbsp. butter
1/2 cup minced chives
8 flounder fillets

3 eggs, beaten lightly
1 cup cornmeal
1/2 cup butter
2 tsp. salt
1/8 tsp. pepper

Scrub mussels, then place on rack in large kettle. Add water, bring to a boil, cover, reduce heat and steam for 15 minutes. Remove mussels from shell and chop finely. Reserve 1/3 cup cooking water. Melt in the 2 tablespoons butter, saute chives and mussels and add mussel liquid. Keep warm over low heat until fillets are browned. Dip fillets in egg then in cornmeal to form a light coating. Brown fillets on both sides in the 1/2 cup butter. Sprinkle with salt and pepper to taste. Serve browned fillets on a large platter topped with mussel sauce.

FRIED RAINBOW TROUT

6 trout (each about 1/2 lb.)
3 eggs, lightly beaten
2 cups cornmeal

1 tsp. salt
1/4 tsp. pepper
3 tbsp. butter

Dip each trout in beaten egg, then in mixture of cornmeal, salt and pepper to coat. Heat butter in fry pan and fry trout for 4 to 5 minutes on each side.

BROILED RAINBOW TROUT

6 trout (each about 1/2 lb)
3 tbsp. butter
1/2 tsp. salt

1/8 tsp. pepper
1/4 cup minced parsley

Rub each fish well with butter. Broil for 4 to 5 minutes per side. Baste with the drippings, season with salt and pepper and top with minced parsley.

STEAMED POMPANO WITH GRAPES

4 lbs. pompano
2 tbsp. butter
1 lb. muscadine grapes

1/2 tsp. salt
1/4 tsp. pepper

Place cleaned fish on large piece of aluminum foil in a baking pan. Rub inside and outside of fish with butter, stuff with halved, seeded grapes and sprinkle inside and out with salt and pepper. Cover with a second large piece of aluminum foil and seal edges. Bake at 400°F for 30 minutes. Loosen top piece of foil, baste with drippings, reseal and steam for 15 minutes. Baste once more before serving.

CODFISH BALLS

2 3/4 lbs. fresh cod
1 quart potatoes, diced
2 tbsp. butter

2 cups water
2 tsp. salt
1/4 tsp. pepper

Combine ingredients and boil, covered, for 25 minutes. Drain well and mash, roll into 2 inch balls and deep fry.

BAKED SEA BASS WITH CHESTNUTS

A 4-lb sea bass
1 tsp. salt
1 scallion, sliced
1 clove garlic, minced
1 cup chopped mushrooms
2 tbsp. oil

1 cup grated apples
2 cups chopped shrimp
1 cup chopped chestnuts
1 cup bread crumbs
1/4 tsp. pepper
3/4 cup apple cider

Sprinkle bass inside and out with salt. Saute scallion, garlic, and mushrooms in oil until golden and combine with remaining ingredients except cider. Lay fish on large piece of aluminum foil and wrap, leaving a small vent at the top for basting. Place wrapped fish in baking pan and bake at 350°F for 1 hour, basting frequently with the apple cider.

SHRIMP AND OKRA STEW

1 lb. okra, sliced
6 tomatoes, chopped
1 bay leaf, crumbled
10 peppercorns
1 tsp. salt

1 cup water
1 1/2 lbs shrimp
1/2 tsp. gumbo file
1 tbsp. water

Place okra, tomatoes, bay leaf, peppercorns, salt and the 1 cup water in a large kettle and simmer, covered, for 20 minutes or until tomatoes have broken up and okra is tender. Add shrimp and gumbo file mixed with the 1 tablespoon water; simmer 10 minutes and serve.

HUPA HALIBUT WITH EGGS

As traditionally prepared, this recipe was cooked in watertight baskets or cedar boxes into which hot stones were dropped to make the water boil. The eggs used were seabird eggs collected from nests built in coastal cliffs. Halibut was a particularly important food source for the Tlingits, who made special halibut hooks with shafts carved with figures that had magical power.

2 cups chicken broth
1 small onion, chopped
1/2 tsp. salt
1/8 tsp. pepper

6 juniper berries, crushed
4 halibut fillets
1 cup seaweed
3 eggs, lightly beaten

Bring broth to a boil, add onion, salt, pepper, and juniper berries. Simmer 15 minutes. Add halibut, but in bite-sized pieces. Simmer 10 minutes. Add seaweed and drizzle in beaten eggs. Cook until eggs are set up.

SMOKED EEL STEW

Eels were a favorite food among Eastern tribes. They were taken from rivers and used fresh, as well as being smoked or dried for winter eating. They were broiled on sapling sticks or mixed into think soups as in this recipe.

1 1/2 lbs. smoked eel	6 cups boiling water
4 yellow onions	1 tsp. salt
4 potatoes	1/8 tsp. pepper

Cut eel into 2-inch pieces, slice onions, cube potatoes and add to the boiling water. Add salt and pepper and simmer for about 1 hour. Skim off excess fat and serve.

CHIPPEWA DILL JELLIED EEL

A 3-lb eel	10 peppercorns
2 tbsp. coarse salt	2 tsp. salt
2 1/2 cups water	2 bay leaves
1/4 cup white wine	2 tbsp. fresh dill
2 wild onions, minced	1/4 cup lemon juice

Skin the eel by cutting around the neck behind the fins. Wrap the head in a piece of paper towel, pull skin back to towel using pliers. Slit eel open, remove entrails and cut eel into 2-inch pieces. Wash well under running water. Arrange eel pieces in a single layer in a shallow pan. Sprinkle with coarse salt and pour in enough water to cover eel completely. Soak 10 minutes, drain and rinse well in running water. Place eel in fireproof casserole. Add the water, wine, onions and seasonings (except lemon juice) and bring to a boil over high heat. Reduce heat and simmer for 20 minutes. Remove from heat and stir in lemon juice. Chill. When thoroughly chilled, the liquid should form a soft jelly. Serve from casserole.

RED SNAPPER WITH ORANGES

2lbs. red snapper	1/8 tsp. pepper
2 tbsp. butter	4 oranges, sliced
2 tbsp. chopped parsley	

Place fish in large baking pan, dot well with butter and sprinkle with parsley and pepper. Lay the orange slices over the fish. Bake at 400°F for 20 minutes. Reduce heat to 350°F and bake 20 minutes more or until fish flakes at the touch of a fork.

SPICY MARINADE FISH BAKE

1 cup lemon juice
1 tbsp. minced onion
3 cloves garlic, mashed
2 tsp. red chili powder

2 tsp. oregano
1 tbsp. salt
3 large trout

Combine all ingredients except front; mix thoroughly. Let stand 15 minutes. Marinate trout in mixture for at least 30 minutes on each side. Wrap trout in cheesecloth, wetting cloth with any remaining marinade. Wrap in foil. Bake fish at 350°F for 1 1/2 hours.

PEROK

1/2 cup butter
Pinch of salt
2 cups flour
1 tbsp. water (approximately)
Half a salmon, cooked and
   flaked

4 onions chopped
4 cooked rutabagas, cubed
2 cups cooked rice
2 eggs, lightly beaten
Salt and pepper to taste

Make a pie crust by cutting butter and salt into flour until mixture forms oatmeal-sized particles. Add enough water to ball up the dry flour. Chill; roll into top and bottom crusts.

Place bottom crust in pie pan and fill with a mixture of the remaining ingredients. Place top crust on, and seal crusts together, bake at 375°F for 45 minutes.

DULSE-SHELLFISH STEW

   Dulse is a pinkish-red seaweed that grows on submerged rocks and ledges. It is a mineral-rich sea plant that is still widely used by coastal tribes.

2 cups dulse
10 cups water
2 onions, chopped
1 cup chopped celery
5 potatoes, cubed

2 cloves garlic, minced
2 bay leaves
2 tsp. salt
5 lbs. periwinkles, mussels,
   clams, crab legs, shrimp

Sear dulse in skillet; set aside. Bring the water to a boil, add all ingredients except shellfish and dulse. Cook until nearly tender. Add shellfish and dulse. Cook 10 minutes.

For the annual Midewiwin Grand Medicine Dance, medicine men of the Chippewa carried elongated pouches of weasel or marten skin filled with white shells called migis. It was the sacred migis which transmitted the spirit power, and a touch from the medicine bags during Midewiwin would cause a person to fall to the ground unconscious.

OYSTER AND SNAPPER STEW

2 tbsp. butter
1 onion, chopped
4 cups chicken bouillon
12-16 small new potatoes
1 medium green apple
1 tbsp. lemon juice

3-4 lbs. red snapper
24 oysters (about 2 cups)
2 cups milk
1/2 tsp. celery seed
1 tbsp. fresh tarragon

Melt butter in large pan, saute onion until translucent, add bouillon and potatoes. Raise heat to high and cook about 7 minutes or until potatoes are done. Cut apple into 1/4-inch julienne sticks and toss with lemon juice to prevent discoloring. Set aside. Add snapper, cut in 2-inch cubes, to soup, lower heat and simmer 10 minutes until done. Add oysters and milk and bring to a boil. Immediately remove from heat; add celery seeds and tarragon. Serve sprinkled with apple sticks.

SCALLOPS WITH GINGER AND MINT

1 tbsp. minced ginger
5 scallions, sliced
1/4 cup butter
2 lbs. small bay scallops

2 carrots, finely grated
2 tbsp. chopped mint
1/2 tsp. salt
1/4 tsp. pepper

Saute ginger and scallions in butter until tender. Add scallops a few at a time, cooking approximately 2 minutes per batch. Set aside. Add carrots, stir, cover and cook until softened (about 15 minutes). Return scallops to pan with mint and seasonings. Remove immediately from heat once scallops are warmed through.

BROILED SHRIMP

4 1/2 lbs. shrimp
1 3/4 cup water
2 tsp. salt
4 cloves garlic, crushed

1/2 cup oil
1/4 tsp. oregano
1/4 tsp. pepper

Place shrimp in large kettle with the water; add 1 teaspoon of the salt. Steam shrimp for 20 minutes and drain, reserving 1 cup of broth. Mix garlic, oil, oregano, pepper, and remaining salt. Shell and devein shrimp. Place on broiler pan, pour garlic mixture over shrimp and broil for 5 minutes. Turn shrimp, pour shrimp broth over them and broil 2 minutes longer, basting with broth. Top each serving with a little of the broth.

SHELLFISH BAKE SEAWEED

Assorted shellfish

Dig a pit 4 feet square and 4 feet deep. Line the pit with stones and build a large fire and keep hot for 4 hours. Brush coals aside and cover rocks with a 4-inch layer of seaweed. Lay shellfish-clams, mussels, periwinkles, sea urchins and crab-on seaweed layer. Cover seafood with a 6-inch layer of seaweed. Lay branches or brush on seaweed to hold in steam. The shellfish should be cooked in about an hour but can be left for as long as 2 hours before eating.

Note: A slight variation on the shellfish bake was used by the Klallam tribe. Upon finding a limpet-covered rock, they covered it with seaweed, which they heaped with hot stones. The limpets loosened their hold on the rock as they cooked and were either eaten on the spot or scraped off and taken home.

PAN-FRIED PERCH

4 perch (more if small)
Flour
Salt and pepper

Butter and shortening (equal amounts)

Shake fish in a bag with flour, salt and pepper, coating thoroughly. Melt butter and shortening in a skillet. Cook fish over a bush fire until brown on both sides. Serve while crisp and hot with butter or tartar sauce.

BASS FILLETS AND STUFFED OLIVES

6 bass fillets
Salt and pepper
1/2 cup dry white wine
3 tbsp. oil
2 onions, sliced
12 stuffed olives

1 tbsp. chopped pimento
2 ripe tomatoes, sliced
1 tbsp. vinegar
1 tsp. salt
Parsley

Arrange fillets in buttered baking dish and season with salt and pepper. Pour the wine around the fillets.

Heat oil in skillet; add onions and saute for 5 minutes. Add olives, pimento, tomatoes, vinegar and salt. Simmer for 20 minutes longer. Spread the sauce over the fillets and bake at 350°F for 30 minutes. When ready to serve, sprinkle with parsley.

FRESH BASS SOUP

3 slices boiled salt pork
2 lbs. bass, filleted
2 cups sliced potatoes
1 large onion, sliced thin

1 1/2 cups hot milk
1 tsp. savory
2 tbsp. butter or margarine

Cut salt pork into 1 1/2-inch squares and brown in a skillet; set aside. Cut fish into 1-inch pieces. Make alternate layers of potatoes, onions and fish in a kettle. Add salt pork and cover with water and bring to a boil. Reduce heat and simmer for 15 minutes, or until potatoes are tender. Add milk, savory and butter. Do not mix; simply keep warm until ready to serve.

CARP IN BEER

4 lbs. carp fillets, cut into serving
    pieces
Salt
3 cups beer
2 onions, sliced
1 bay leaf

6 peppercorns
1 lemon, sliced
1 tbsp. flour
1 tbsp. butter
1 tbsp. sugar

Sprinkle fish with salt and let it sit for 1/2 hour. Place fish in a saucepan. Pour in beer and add onions, bay leaf, peppercorns, and lemon. Simmer until fish is tender, about 30 to 45 minutes. Remove fish to platter. Make a paste of flour and butter and stir into broth. Add sugar and simmer until hot. Pour sauce over fish. Serve.

CATFISH BAKE

3 tbsp. butter or margarine
1/2 cup flour
1/2 tsp. dry mustard
1/8 tsp. tarragon

1/4 tsp. marjoram
6 or 7 catfish, skinned and
    cleaned
1 cup evaporated milk

Melt butter in a baking dish. Mix flour with mustard, tarragon and marjoram. Dip fish in milk, then roll in flour mixture. Lay fish in hot butter. Bake at 325°F for 15 to 20 minutes. Remove from oven and turn fish over. Place back in oven for another 15 to 20 minutes. Serve on a hot platter.

SKILLET-FRIED CATFISH

6 catfish, skinned, cleaned
1/2 tsp. salt
1/4 tsp. pepper

1/2 cup canned milk
1/2 cup cornmeal
1/2 cup bacon fat

Sprinkle the insides of the fish with salt and pepper. Dip fish, first in milk, then into cornmeal. Melt bacon fat in a heavy skillet and fry fish until golden brown on one side, about 4 to 5 minutes. Turn carefully and fry the other side, until fish flakes easily when tested with a fork. Serve with favorite sauce.

CATFISH DELIGHT

8 catfish
Prepared mustard

1 cup flour
Bacon fat

Fillet fish and wash in cold water. Pat dry. Spread mustard on both sides of the fillets. Dredge with flour and fry in hot bacon fat until golden brown.

CATFISH STEW

2 slices bacon, chopped
1 large onion, chopped
1 large can tomatoes
1 cup boiling water
2 large potatoes, diced
2 tbsp. Worcestershire sauce

1/4 cup catsup
1 tsp. salt
1/4 tsp. thyme
1 1/2 lbs. skinned catfish, cut in
   bite-sized pieces

In a heavy saucepan or Dutch oven, fry bacon and onions. Then add tomatoes, water, and other ingredients (except fish). Cover and simmer for 30 minutes. Add fish and cook, uncovered, for 15 minutes.

CASSEROLE OF EEL

A 3-lb eel
Salted water
1/2 cup flour
1 tsp. salt
1/8 tsp. pepper

1/4 cup butter
12 small peeled onions
1 bay leaf
2 cups water
1 cup mushrooms

Skin and clean the eel thoroughly and cut in 3-inch pieces. Soak in cold salted water for 1 hour. Drain and pat dry. Dredge in flour. Sprinkle with salt and pepper. Then brown in melted butter. Put eel in a casserole dish and add onions, bay leaf and the water. Cover and bake at 350°F for 35 minutes. Add mushrooms and cook for another 25 minutes.

MUSKELLUNGE

1 muskellunge, filleted
1 cup pancake mix
Water
Salt and pepper to taste

Garlic powder
Onion powder
Fat for frying

Cut the muskie fillets into serving pieces. Using commercial pancake mix add enough water to make a batter. Mix salt, pepper, garlic powder and onion powder into the batter. Heat oil in a wok. Dip fish in batter and then place in wok. Turn once and cook until both sides are a deep golden brown. Serve.

MUSKIE STEAKS

1 muskellunge, dressed
Salt and pepper to taste

Italian salad dressing
Melted butter

Cut muskie into thin steaks. Make marinade by combining salt, pepper and Italian salad dressing. Marinate the steaks for a few hours, turning once after 1 hour. Lightly grease a shallow broiling pan. Place steaks on broiler pan and broil until golden brown on each side. Baste with a combination of melted butter and marinade. Place on platter and pour remaining butter and marinade over steaks. Serve.

When it was time for the Mandan of the Northeastern Plains to move camp, they would use "Bull Boats." The hide of a single buffalo was stretched across a wooden frame, leaving the tail on for a rudder. Then, they would paddle themselves and their belongings to the new location.

BAKED MUSKELLUNGE

1 muskellunge, filleted
Salt and pepper to taste
Garlic powder
Melted butter

Lemon juice
Onion, chopped finely
Grated cheese

Line a baking dish with foil, leaving enough foil to fold over and seal in the fish. Cut fillets into service-sized pieces and season with salt, pepper and garlic powder. Brush foil with butter and lemon juice and place fish in dish. Sprinkle onion over the fish and pour butter and lemon juice over top. Fold over the foil and bake at 350°F for 45 minutes. Peel back foil and sprinkle with grated cheese. Put back in oven just until cheese melts. Serve.

PICKEREL 'N' SAUCE

1 lb. pickerel, in serving pieces
Flour
1 tsp. salt
1/2 tsp. pepper

2 tbsp. bacon drippings
1 medium onion, diced
1 can (10 oz.) mushroom soup
1/2 cup milk

Wash fillets and pat dry then dredge with flour. Sprinkle on salt and pepper. In a skillet, melt bacon drippings, then add fillets to brown on all sides. Add onion, mushroom soup and milk; cover and cook over medium heat for 30 minutes.

PICKEREL BISQUE

Fish to serve 4
4 cups fish stock
3 tbsp. butter
1 tbsp. flour
Sprig of thyme

1 cup heavy cream
14 tsp. parsley
Salt and pepper
Crumbled crackers

Fillet the fish. Make a fish stock, using heads, tails and bones. Strain stock, add fillets, and simmer until they flake. Remove fish and chop fine. In a saucepan, melt butter; stir in the flour until smooth. Stir in the stock and the thyme and bring to a boil; then add fish, cream, parsley, salt and pepper to taste. Heat thoroughly, pour over the crackers and serve.

PICKEREL SOUP

2 lbs. filleted pickerel
2 tbsp. butter or margarine
2 tbsp. cooking oil
1 large carrot, grated
1 large onion, minced
2 tomatoes, peeled and sliced

2 quarts boiling water
1 cup uncooked noodles
1/4 tsp. thyme
1/4 tsp. savory
1 tsp. salt
1/2 tsp. pepper

Cut fish into serving pieces. Put butter, oil, carrots, onions, and tomatoes in large pan and simmer for 10 minutes. Add water and noodles. Bring to a boil, then reduce heat and add thyme, savory, salt and pepper. Carefully add fish and simmer for 20 minutes.

PIKEBURGER

1 egg
1/2 tsp. salt
1/4 tsp. pepper
Pinch each of tarragon, thyme
    and parsley

1 1/2 to 2 lbs. ground pike
1 onion, chopped fine
1 tsp. lemon juice
1 cup bread crumbs
Bacon fat

Combine egg, salt, pepper and seasonings. Mix in pike, onion, lemon juice and bread crumbs. Shape into patties and fry in bacon fat as you would hamburgers.

BROILED OPEN PIKE

1 pike
Salt and pepper
2 tbsp. lemon juice

Butter
1 cup dry white wine

Split the fish lengthwise. Place fish in a buttered broiler pan, skin side down. Sprinkle with salt and pepper. Baste fish with half of lemon juice and butter and place under broiler, about 6 inches away from heat. Add remaining lemon juice to wine; baste fish frequently with mixture. Fish is done when it flakes easily with a fork.

PIKE CASSEROLE

2 lbs. filleted pike, cut in pieces
4 large potatoes, peeled and
   sliced

1 large onion, chopped
4 slices bacon, chopped
Salt and pepper to taste

Lightly grease baking dish and alternate layers of fish, potatoes and onions, beginning and ending with potatoes. Distribute chopped bacon over each layer. Sprinkle with salt and pepper. Cover the mixture with cold water. Cover and bake at 350°F for 35 to 40 minutes.

SALMON LOAF

2 cups boiled salmon
1/2 cup bread crumbs
1/2 tsp. baking powder
3 eggs, beaten
1/4 cup melted butter

1/2 cup cream
2 tbsp. lemon juice
1 tbsp. chopped parsley
1 tsp. grated lemon rind

Mix all ingredients together, blending very well. Pour mixture into a greased loaf pan. Bake at 350°F for 30 minutes.

SALMON RICE SALAD

1 1/2 cups cooked rice
1/4 cup French dressing
3/4 cup mayonnaise
1 tbsp. finely chopped onion
1 tsp. horseradish sauce
1/2 tsp. chopped celery

1 cup cooked salmon
Half a cucumber, peeled and
   sliced
1 hard-boiled egg, diced
1/2 tsp. celery salt
1/2 tsp. salt

While rice is still hot, add French dressing. Cool to room temperature before adding remaining ingredients. Mix lightly. Chill for 1 hour before serving.

MACARONI SALMON CASSEROLE

2 cups cooked salmon
4 cups cooked macaroni
1 medium onion, chopped
Salt and pepper to taste

1 can (10 oz.) mushroom or
    celery soup
1/2 cup milk or water
1 cup cracker crumbs

In a casserole dish, combine the salmon, macaroni, onion, salt and pepper. Mix in the soup and the milk or water. Sprinkle the top with the cracker crumbs and dot with margarine. Bake at 350°F for 45 minutes.

✳ CHAPTER FIVE ✳

CLEANING & SKINNING OF FISH AND GAME; TANNING

Before any recipe can begin, the cleaning and skinning process must be completed.

On the following pages you will find the information you need to clean, skin, and tan the various animals mentioned in our recipes as well as to clean and prepare fowl and fish.

Also included you will find cleaning and preparation guides for fowl and fish.

CLEANING AND SKINNING OF BIG GAME ANIMALS

For deer and other big game animals, quick cleaning and cooling is of the utmost importance. First of all, lay the deer with its head downhill and cut the throat so that it will bleed thoroughly. Lay the deer flat on its back and slit the belly all the way down to within 6 inches of the tail, being careful not to cut the intestine. Make a circular cut completely around the vent to free it and the large intestine. Next, cut the windpipe. Then cut the diaphragm, which separates the chest from the abdominal cavity. Now grab the front legs and give it a jerk and roll the deer over; the insides will spill out on the ground. Cut off the heart and the liver and save. Do all this quickly and thoroughly. In case of punctured organs, there will be bleeding, which causes contamination.

The carcass should be cooled quickly. If the weather prevents this, rub the inside with black pepper. This will keep the flies away. Prop the carcass open with a stick so that the air will circulate. If there is a part of the meat which has been badly shot up, it should be cut away. If its condition isn't too bad, you can soak it overnight in a brine to remove the blood and then use it for venison burgers.

When you skin the deer, hang it up by the hind feet and cut the hide around the ankles. Make cuts from the inner thighs to the vent. Pull the skin down. It may be so firmly adhered that you will need to use a knife to loosen it.

HOW TO SKIN A FISH

Make a cut along the dorsal fins, the lower edge of the belly and just behind the gills. Holding the head of the fish with the left hand, take the upper left corner of the skin in a pair of pliers an pull it toward you. Repeat this on the other side, then remove head and entrails. Wash fish thoroughly inside and out with cold water. You will find that blood clings to the backbone but can be removed by scrubbing with a small brush. Shake salt inside the cavity along the backbone. A few small gashes along the backbone will prevent the fish from curling in the skillet.

HOW TO FILLET A FISH

Cut through the skin from the head to tail along the backbone on each side of the dorsal fin. Cut a V-shaped notch behind the head, cutting to the backbone. Cut through the skin and pull it toward the tail, holding the fish in your hand. Cut to the backbone. Turn the knife to a horizontal position and slide it along the backbone, cutting off the flesh in one slab. Turn the fish, and repeat on the other side. If the fish tends to slip away from you, you can nail the head to a board. Check the fillet for any bones and wash thoroughly with cold water.

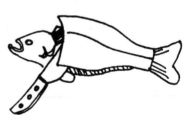

SKINNING AND DRESSING OF SMALL GAME ANIMALS

BEAVER

Lay beaver on its back and cut off legs at the first joint. Cut pelt in a straight line down the chest and belly to vent. Pull skin from flesh, being careful when you pull legs through the skin. Cut off tail and head.

Make a cut through the layer of meat from the breastbone to the vent, encircling the vent. Lay body cavity open and remove the entrails. Carefully cut out tiny mush glands from under the skin on the inside of legs, and be sure to remove the castor gland under the belly near the tail. Trim off all fat. Wash and soak meat in warm salted water.

BEAVER TAILS

Wash thoroughly. Roast until skin begins to blister. Remove; cool; peel skin off. You may now roast or boil in salted water until tender.

FROG LEGS

Cut the legs from the frog. Wash them, and peel the skin back so it will come off rather like a glove. Cut off the feet. Pour boiling water over the legs; drain and dry them. Now they are ready to cook.

GROUNDHOG

Dress groundhog as you would for beaver, but watch for and remove 7 to 9 small sacs or kernels in the small of the back and under the forearms. Wash and soak carcass in warm salted water.

MUSKRAT

Slit skin on the inside of the hind legs, from the paws to the vent, and cut off both hind and forepaws and tail. Then work skin off inside out. Remove head from the carcass. Insert knife at the tip of breastbone and slit muskrat down the front. Open body cavity and remove the entrails. Cut out musk glands from inside the legs, plus white tissuey skin and all fat. Wash and soak meat in warm salted water.

MUSKRAT TAILS

Cut off the tails and dip them into very hot water. Pull off the fur. One can either cook them on the top of the stove, turning them after a few minutes, or boil them.

This is the same method as for beaver tails. Both tails are very sticky to eat.

RABBIT

To dress rabbit, cut front legs at the first joint. Cut through skin around hind legs. Tie hind legs together and hang rabbit. Pull skin down off the hind legs and peel it off, inside out, over the body and forelegs. Cut head off. Slit rabbit down the front and remove the entrails. Wash meat with warm water.

RACCOON

Skin by cutting around the hind legs and the inside of the thigh to the crotch. Loosen the skin and work toward head. When you have reached the head, you can cut off the head and feet. Cut a slit down the belly and remove the entrails. Wash and soak in warm salted water.

PORCUPINE

To ready the porcupine for cleaning, first the quills have to be removed. To do this, you burn the quills off and then scrape right done to the hide. This method adds to the flavor of the meat. Otherwise, the cleaning and skinning process would be the same method as is for the raccoon, ground hog and other small game animals.

The porcupine is at its best when trapped and cooked in September.

TURTLE

Remove the head form the turtle and hang the shell neck down on a hook for 1/2 hour until the blood stops dripping. Then wash the turtle and drop it into boiling water and cook for 10 minutes. Pour off the water and cover the turtle with cold water. Let it stand until cooked enough to handle. Rub the nails and black skin from the legs with a towel.

Wash the turtle carefully and place it in a pot. Cover it with boiling water and simmer until the flesh is tender. This will be when the joints of the legs can be broken with slight pressure and the shell easily separates. This will take 50 to 60 minutes. Remove the turtle from the water, cool and place turtle on its back with the head end away from you. Loosen and remove the under shell. The liver, gall bladder and sand bag will be found near the head end, the gall being attached to the left side of the liver. Take out the gall as you would that of a chicken, being careful not to break it. Remove the entrails and throw them away. Then take out the eggs, if any. Remove the slight membrane and drop the eggs in cold water. Cut all the meat very fine.

DRESSING OF GAME BIRDS

If you are not able to pluck your bird in the field, at least clean it as much as possible. Cut the throat and hang it head-down to bleed. Remove the feathers from the crop and tail, pulling them gently toward the tail so as not to break the skin. Slit the skin up over the crop and remove it. Cut down to the vent and remove the entrails, separating the giblets and putting them back in the cavity or in a separate bag. Carefully cut away the oil sac at the base of the tail.

It is much easier to pluck a bird that is thoroughly chilled. To pluck, pick all pin feathers from a bird. After removing the coarser feathers, if those remaining are downy or small, you may use the paraffin method. Make a mixture of 2 gallons of boiling water with 1/2 pound of melted paraffin wax. Dip the duck so it becomes coated with wax, it will take several dips to build up a sufficiently thick coat. Let the paraffin wax cool and harden. You may scrape it off with a dull knife or you may roll it off with your fingers.

It may be advisable to skin the bird, if the skin has been badly torn by shooting. Cut through the skin over the breast and peel the skin and peel the remainder of the skin and feathers from the bird.

TANNING FURS AND LEATHERS

ANIMAL	USE	COMMENT
Bear	rugs	hard, durable
Beaver	coats	wears well
Deer	gloves, coats, moccasins	wears very well, soft, pliable
Muskrat	coats	wears well
Rabbit	gloves	fairly delicate
Raccoon	hats, coats	wears well
Squirrel	coat	delicate fur
Groundhog	gloves	delicate fur

EQUIPMENT AND SUPPLIES NEEDED

Skinning knife to remove hide (a regular knife may be used but it must be razor sharp).
Rubber gloves
Plastic and wooden containers
Wooden stir stick
Neat's-foot oil or corn oil

Salt or borax

Fleshing knife, butcher knife or draw knife

Hydrated lime, for dehairing

Alum

Oatmeal or hardwood sawdust

Sandpaper

STEP-BY-STEP TANNING INSTRUCTIONS

1. Remove the hide from the animal; being careful neither to cut through the skin nor to leave big chunks of flesh on the animal.

2 (a). Fleshing. Once the hide has been removed from the animal, fleshing involves removing bits of meat and fat that are still on the hide. To make the job easier, first soak the skin in a salt or borax solution using the following proportions:

1 pound salt per 2 gallons of soft water

1 ounce borax per gallon of water

(Note: Use hot water to dissolve the borax but let it cool off before immersing the skin).

An agitator type washing machine will speed up the soaking process and also help reduce hair loss by avoiding oversoaking. Soak for about 12 hours or overnight. Remove from solution and rinse in fresh water and let drain. Then while the flesh side is still moist, rub in the salt until the flesh side is completely covered (avoid getting salt onto the fur side.).

When the first application has soaked in, apply a second. Fold the hide in half lengthwise, flesh side to flesh side; then troll it up and place on a slanted surface so that it can drain.

Begin fleshing the next day. Place the hide fur side down on a smooth log and scrape away the fat and gristle with a fleshing knife, butcher knife, or drawknife. Scrape carefully and evenly. The membrane on the hide's inner surface must be removed for tanning to be successful. Scrape with the blunt edge occasionally to help soften the leather. After fleshing is complete, wash the hide in a soapy solution, then rinse quickly and thoroughly.

2 (b). Dehairing. If you wish to remove the hair, it is necessary to soak the hide in a dehairing solution. Use 1 pound of hydrated lime per 8 gallons of soft water and soak for about 5 days, stirring twice a day or longer if the weather is cold, in a wooden or plastic container. (Lime is caustic). When the hair is loose, rinse the hide. Then place it fur side up on a smooth log and scrape off the hair and loose surface skin with the dull edge of your felting knife. When all the hair is removed, then proceed to tan.

3. Tanning. The solution that we will give here has certain advantages over some of the other methods:

- The hide will not overtan.

- The solution contains no dangerous acids or toxic vapors.

Nevertheless, it is still necessary to use rubber gloves. In a large plastic or wooden container, add 5 pounds of salt to 10 gallons of warm soft water (rain water will do). Next mix 2 pounds alum in enough hot water to dissolve it. Then mix the 2 solutions together, stirring with a wooden paddle until the ingredients are thoroughly mixed. The solution can be used warm or cold but not hot. Immerse the hide in the tanning solution and stir gently about twice a day.

Make certain the solution reaches every nook and cranny in the hide, the larger the hide, the longer it takes to tan. For example a rabbit takes about 2 days and a deer takes about 7 days. To test for complete tanning, cut off a little bit of the hide and if the color is uniform all the way through, the hide is tanned. It is very important to tan completely.

4. When the hide is tanned, remove it from the solution and rinse it either with a garden hose or in a sink with many changes of water.

5. Next hang it over something out of direct sunlight and in such a way that the air can circulate around the hide.

6. After several days, while the hair and hide are still damp, fold the hide flesh side to flesh side and roll it up. Leave it like this overnight.

If the hide dried before you were able to roll it up, use a wet sponge to dampen the flesh side before you roll it up.

7. Work the hide by stretching and pulling it over a smooth surface; continue in this manner until the hide is pliable.

8. When the hide is pliable, with the tips of your fingers, rub in the neat's-foot oil, or corn oil on the flesh side. Use warm oil.

9. To clean the fur side, fill a plastic bag with oatmeal or hardwood sawdust and shake until fur is clean.

10. Brush and comb fur until it is entirely fluffed up. Use coarse sandpaper on any rough spots on flesh side.

THE HIDE IS NOW READY TO USE

✳ CHAPTER SIX ✳
WILD RICE

Wild rice ripens in August. It usually grows in moving waters about 3 to 4 feet deep. The very long, seed-like grass is often 8 to 10 feet tall and has a long brown flower on top. To harvest, bind the plant over your canoe and beat the pulp, causing the fruit to fall into the canoe.

To preserve wild rice, first spread out in a warm place until it is thoroughly dried. Then, bake in a shallow pan for about 2 hours at 225°F, stirring occasionally, to parch it evenly.

After drying, the husk can be loosened by pounding and rubbing through the hands. Store in jars and seal. Always wash the rice thoroughly before using; otherwise it has a disagreeable smoky flavor.

✳

In addition to wild rice, another staple of the Menominee was the Spikenard. Its roots were gathered and sliced, then cooked along with wild onions and gooseberries.

BAKED WILD RICE

Half a medium onion, minced
1/4 cup butter
1 cup wild rice

2 cups homemade chicken stock
2 tbsp. butter
Salt

Saute onion with the 1/4 cup butter in a Dutch oven. Add rice and stir until well mixed. Bring chicken stock to a boil in a saucepan; add to rice. Cover tightly and bake for 25 minutes. Mix rice gently with the 2 tablespoons butter and salt to stock. Serve.

WILD RICE SPOON BREAD

1 cup cooked wild rice
1/4 cup corn meal
2 cups buttermilk
1/2 tsp. baking soda

1 tsp. salt
2 eggs, beaten
2 tbsp. melted butter

Combine ingredients one at a time in order given. Put batter in a greased baking dish and bake at 325°F for 1 hour.

QUICK WILD RICE DISH

1/2 cup chopped onions
1/4 lb. mushrooms, sliced
2 tbsp. butter
1 tbsp. flour
1/2 cup beef bouillon

1/2 tsp. salt
1/2 tsp. pepper
2 cups (cooked) wild rice
1/2 cup chopped parsley
1/4 cup chopped almonds

Saute onions and mushrooms in butter. Stir in flour. Add bouillon and simmer, stirring frequently, till smooth. Add seasonings, wild rice, parsley and almonds. Serve.

SPEEDY WILD RICE PUDDING

1 package (4 serving size) instant
    vanilla pudding
2 cups milk

Dash nutmeg
1 1/2 cups cooked wild rice
1/4 cup raisins, cooked

Prepare pudding as directed with the milk, adding nutmeg. Mix in cooled rice and raisins. Chill for 15 minutes before serving.

STIR-FRIED WILD RICE 'N VEGETABLES

1/2 cup wild rice
1 1/2 cups boiling water
1 clove garlic, sliced
3 tbsp. vegetable oil
4 green onions, sliced
1 stalk celery, sliced

1 cup of bean sprouts
2 tbsp. soy sauce
1/4 tsp. ginger
1/4 tsp. pepper
2 cups spinach leaves

Wash wild rice; stir into the boiling water. Simmer for 25 minutes, covered. Drain. Saute garlic in oil for 5 minutes. Remove garlic. Stir-fry onions and celery in oil 5 minutes. Add bean sprouts, cooked wild rice, soy sauce, ginger and pepper. Stir-fry for 5 minutes. Add spinach leaves and stir-fry for 2 minutes.

BAKED WILD RICE AND CARROTS

1 1/2 cups wild rice, washed in
    cold water
2 1/2 cups water
2 1/2 tsp. salt
4 slices bacon, cut into strips

1 onion, peeled and chopped
1 cup finely grated carrots
4 mushrooms, chopped
1/2 cup light cream
1 egg

Place the wild rice, water and salt in a large saucepan, and bring to a boil. Boil vigorously for about 10 minutes. Turn off heat, cover, and let rice stand for about 20 minutes or until all the water has been absorbed. Brown the bacon, remove from drippings, and drain on paper toweling. Saute the onions and mushrooms in the bacon drippings until the onions are golden and transparent. Mix the bacon, sauted onions and mushrooms, and grated carrots into the wild rice. Beat the cream and egg until light, and fold into the wild rice mixture. Bake, covered, in a buttered 1 1/2-quart casserole in a moderately slow oven, 325°F for 30 minutes. Remove cover, stir the mixture well with a fork and bake for 15 minutes at the same temperature. Stir once again and bake, uncovered, for 15 minutes longer.

CHIPPEWA WILD RICE

1 cup wild rice, washed in cold
    water
2 1/2 cups water
1 1/2 tsp. salt
4 strips bacon, cut into julienne
    strips

6 eggs
1/4 tsp. pepper
2 tbsp. minced chives
Bacon drippings plus melted
    butter or margarine to
    measure 1/3 cup

Place the wild rice, the water and 1 teaspoon of the salt in a saucepan, and bring slowly to a boil. Reduce heat and simmer, uncovered, until all water is absorbed. Render the bacon in a large, heavy skillet. Drain bacon on paper toweling. Save drippings. Beat eggs, the remaining 1/2 teaspoon salt and the pepper until light. Pour into the skillet in which you browned the bacon, and brown the eggs lightly. Then turn gently, as you would a pancake, and brown on the other side. When eggs are firm, cut into julienne strips. Lightly toss the bacon, julienne egg strips, chives and bacon drippings plus melted butter or margarine with the rice. Serve hot as a main dish.

✳ CHAPTER SEVEN ✳

SAUCES, MARINADES, STUFFINGS, BATTERS AND BREADS

THIN CREAMY SAUCE

1 cup milk
1 tbsp. flour

1 tbsp. fat
1/2 tsp. seasoning

Excellent for a creamy soup base.

MEDIUM WHITE SAUCE

1 cup milk
2 tbsp. flour

1 1/2 tbsp. fat
1/2 tsp. seasoning

Use this sauce for a creamed and scalloped dishes or as a gravy.

TASTY SOUFFLE SAUCE

1 cup milk
3 tbsp. flour

2 tbsp. fat
1 tsp. seasoning

This sauce, and a wise selection of seasoning for the particular dish, is wonderful for various souffles.

THICK CROQUETTE WHITE SAUCE

1 cup milk
1/4 cup flour

2 1/2 tbsp. fat
1 tsp. seasoning

MOOSE MARINADE

1 cup pineapple juice   1/2 tsp. allspice
1/2 cup honey

Combine above ingredients and brush on meat. Fry or roast. The longer meat is left to marinate, the better it will taste.

VENISON MARINADE

1/2 cup salad oil   1/4 cup chopped onion
1/4 cup vinegar   1 tsp. salt
2 tsp. Worcestershire sauce

Combine all ingredients. Let meat stand in marinade for 2 hours at room temperature. If marinade does not fully cover meat, turn meat several times.

SPICY VENISON MARINADE

Combine one part vinegar or lemon juice with three parts salad or olive oil. Season with your preference of spices which might include from the following list:

1/4 tsp. dill seed   1/2 tsp. celery flakes
2 medium onions, sliced   1-2 bay leaves
1/4 tsp. celery seed   1 tsp. parsley flakes
1 clove garlic, crushed   2 carrots, sliced
1/4 tsp. cloves

Note: When marinating meat, cover meat entirely or turn several times and then refrigerate for 4-12 hours.

The Plains tribes would often hang the paunch of a buffalo from a tripod and use it as a stew pot by filling it with water, meat and vegetables, then adding hot stones, one after another, until the stew was cooked.

BARBECUE SAUCE

1 medium onion, chopped
1 clove garlic, minced
2 tbsp. butter or margarine
1/2 cup catsup
1/4 cup water

2 tbsp. vinegar
1 tbsp. brown sugar
1 tsp. salt
1 tsp. dry mustard
1/2 tsp. Tabasco sauce

Saute onion and garlic in butter or margarine until tender. Add remaining ingredients and bring to a boil. Brush on roasts, ribs or steaks.

VENISON STEAK CHASEUR (SAUCE)

2 tbsp. butter
2 tbsp. flour
1 tbsp. tomato paste
3/4 cup consomme

2 tsp. wine or cider vinegar
1 tsp. grape or current jelly
1/2 tsp. salt
1/4 tsp. pepper

Melt butter. Add flour and stir over low heat until lightly browned. Add tomato paste and consomme, then stir until smooth and creamy. Cook over low heat for 1 hour, stirring once or twice. Then add vinegar, jelly, salt and pepper.

EGG SAUCE

2 tbsp. margarine or butter
1 tbsp. flour

1 cup milk
3 hard-boiled eggs, finely sliced

Melt margarine in a saucepan and mix in flour until well blended. Slowly mix in milk and bring to a boil. Stir in eggs and remove pan from heat. Pour sauce over fish and serve.

CREOLE SAUCE

2 medium onions, sliced
1 clove garlic, chopped fine
1 tbsp. chopped parsley
3 tbsp. butter, margarine or oil

3 1/2 cups tomato juice
1/4 tsp. Worcestershire sauce
Salt and pepper to taste

Cook onions, garlic and parsley in fat until onion is golden brown. Add tomato juice and Worcestershire sauce and cook gently for 15 minutes. Season with salt and pepper.

MUSHROOM SAUCE

1/4 cup margarine
1 small minced onion
1-1 1/2 cups sliced mushrooms
1 clove garlic minced

2 cups beef bouillon
1/3 cup all purpose flour
1/2 tsp. each salt and pepper

Melt margarine in a saucepan and saute onion, mushrooms and garlic. Add beef bouillon and increase heat to medium for 10 minutes. Combine flour, salt and pepper. Add mixture to saucepan and gently boil for 5 minutes. Pour heated sauce over meat.

GWAP GIZ GUN

2 cups flour
2 tbsp. baking powder
1/2 tsp. salt

1/2 cup water or buttermilk
Salt

Combine flour, baking powder and salt; then make a well and mix in liquid. Turn out on floured board and knead. Flatten with palm of hand and roll out to 1/2 inch in thickness. Place on back of a woodstove that has been sprinkled with salt. Cook until light brown on one side, then turn over. Do not have stove too hot. When cooked, spread with margarine and sprinkle with salt.

BACON CORNBREAD

1 1/3 cups flour
1 cup cornmeal
1/2 cup sugar
1 1/2 tsp. baking powder
1/2 tsp. baking soda

1 tsp. salt
8 slices cooked bacon, crumbled
1 egg, beaten
1 1/2 cups evaporated milk
1/3 cup bacon drippings

Combine flour, cornmeal, sugar, baking powder, baking soda, salt and crumbled bacon. In a separate bowl combine egg, evaporated milk and bacon drippings. Add to flour mixture and stir just until moistened. Pour into a greased 8 inch square pan. Bake at 350°F for 40-45 minutes. Serve warm with maple syrup.

SHUSWAP BANNOCK

3 cups all-purpose flour
1 tbsp. baking powder
1 1/2 tsp. salt

1 1/2 cups water
1 cup blueberries

Mix dry ingredients together, then add water quickly and continue to stir. Spread on a pie plate, top with blueberries and put in oven at 425°F for 20 minutes.

GRANDMA'S SWEET BISCUITS

3 cups flour
2 tbsp. baking powder
1/2 tsp. salt
1 cup brown sugar

1/2 cup raisins
1/2 lb. lard
1/2 cup water

Combine first four ingredients, then add raisins. Cut lard into flour mixture and stir. Make a well in center; slowly mix in water using only enough to hold dough together. Shape dough into a ball; then turn out onto a floured board. Knead 3 to 4 times, then roll out to 1/2 inch thickness. Cut with a round cutter and bake at 375°F for 35 to 40 minutes.

POTATO SCONES

2 cups flour
1 tsp. salt
1 tbsp. baking powder
1 tbsp. shortening

1 cup cold mashed potatoes
1 egg
1/3 cup milk

Mix together flour, salt and baking powder. Mix in shortening and cold potatoes. Beat egg and stir in milk. Add to potato mixture. Roll 3/8 inch thick on a floured board and cut into squares. Cook slowly in greased frying pan. Turn several times so that cakes brown on both sides.

ALL BRAN BREAD

1 1/2 cups all bran
1 1/2 cups all-purpose flour
1/2 cup white sugar
1 tsp. baking soda

1/2 tsp. salt
1 egg, beaten
1/2 cup molasses
1 1/2 cups sour milk

Combine all dry ingredients and make a well in center. Add egg, molasses and milk. Mix well and pour into a greased loaf pan. Bake at 325°F for 35 to 40 minutes.

Service berries, a common plant in the northeast, were gathered in great quantities. The were beaten into a paste, made into cakes and dried to be used in making bread or, sometimes, pemmican.

WILD RICE STUFFING

2 cups (cooked) wild rice
2 tbsp. crisp crumbled bacon
2/3 cup stewed tomatoes

1/2 tsp. salt
1 tsp. minced onion
1/2 tsp. pepper

Mix all ingredients together. Stuffing is good with fowl.

PARTRIDGE STUFFING

4 cups dried bread, cut in 1/2-
    inch cubes
3/4 finely chopped cup celery,
1/4 cup chopped green pepper
1 finely chopped small onion

1 tbsp. minced parsley
1/2 tsp. salt
1/4 cup butter
2 eggs

Combine bread, celery , pepper, onion, parsley and salt. Melt butter; remove
from heat. Stir in unbeaten eggs and add to bread mixture. Toss lightly.

FRIED BREAD

5 cups all-purpose flour
10 tsp. baking powder
1/4 cup sugar
1/2 tsp. salt

2 tbsp. vegetable oil
2 eggs, beaten
2 cups water

Sift together flour. Baking powder, sugar and salt. In a separate bowl, combine
vegetable oil, eggs and water. Make a well in center of flour mixture and stir in
liquid, mixing well. Put a clean towel over the bowl and let stand for 3 1/2
hours. Knead dough for about 3 minutes. Turn out onto a floured surface and
roll out to 4-inch thickness. Cut pieces in triangular shapes and fry in hot fat
until golden brown.

EASY FISH BATTER

2 eggs, beaten
1/2 cup milk

1 pkg. crushed crackers

Mix together in a bowl eggs and milk. Then on a plate of an appropriate size
spread out cracker crumbs. dip fish pieces in egg and milk mixture. Roll fish in
the crushed cracker crumbs and fry.

CRANBERRY AND RAISIN STUFFING

1 cup chopped fresh cranberries
1/4 cup sugar
1/4 cup melted butter
5 cups fine stale bread crumbs

1/4 cup raisins
1 tsp. grated orange rind
1 tsp. salt

In a bowl mix cranberries and sugar. Allow to set a few minutes. In a separate bowl mix melted butter and crumbs together. Then add sugared cranberries raisins, rind and salt, adding just enough water to bind mixture. Makes enough for 5-to 6-pound birds.

Recipe can be doubled.

CORN BREAD STUFFING

1/4 cup butter
1 onion, diced
2 stalks celery, diced

3 cups crumbled cornbread
1 cup pecans, chopped
1/2 tsp. thyme

Melt butter in skillet. Saute onion and celery until soft. Combine cornbread and pecans in a bowl and toss with the sauteed vegetables and butter from the skillet. Sprinkle with thyme and toss again.

Seven ears of corn were always put aside at harvest time for the next year's planting. It was a practice followed by the Cherokee in order to attract the corn until the new crop ripened and it was time for the Green Corn Dance. The seven ears would then be eaten with the newly harvested crop and seven more ears were set aside for the next year.

CHEESE STUFFING FOR FISH

1 medium onion, chopped
1/4 cup bacon drippings or
    margarine
2 cups bread crumbs
1/2 cup cheese grated

2 tbsp. chopped parsley
2 tbsp. mustard
1/2 tsp. salt
1/4 tsp. pepper

Cook onion in drippings until tender. In a bowl combine bread crumbs, cheese, parsley, mustard, salt and pepper. Add onions and drippings and toss slightly.

HOMEMADE FISH BATTER

1 1/2 cups all-purpose flour
1 tbsp. baking powder
1 tsp. salt

1 cup milk
2 eggs, well beaten

Mix and sift dry ingredients. Add milk to eggs. Pour liquid into dry mixture, and beat until smooth. Dip fish pieces into mixture and deep-fry in oil or fat until golden brown.

✳ CHAPTER EIGHT ✳
EDIBLE WILD PLANTS, BERRIES, AND WILD BAKING

ABOUT WILD PLANTS

There are hundreds of wild plants that are good to eat. Indians relied on these various plants for many of their basic food staples.

The illustrations provided here are a general aid to identification only. Do not attempt to eat something new to you based on these illustrations alone. Many different plants appear the same to the untrained eye. Please consult with an experienced friend or other resource person before eating a plant for the first time. Never eat anything you are unsure about.

Red Clover

CLOVER, RED (*TRIFOLIUM PRATENSE*)

These plants should be picked in the spring. The rose-pink flowers are about 1 inch long and are formed in dense globe-shaped heads.

CLOVER, WHITE (*TRIFOLIUM REPENS*)

These flowers are white with pink bases, and the leaflets are heart-shaped and formed in groups of three.

The roots, stems and flowers of the clover are all edible, but as with all wild flowers, should

White Clover

be cleaned and soaked in salted water for a couple of hours. Use in favorite recipe, as directed.

LAMB'S QUARTERS (*CHENOPODIUM ALBUM*)

These plants should be gathered in spring or early summer. The leaves are diamond-shaped and toothed. A pale green flower grows at the top of the plant in clusters. The flavor of lambs' quarters suggests that of spinach and as with spinach, when preparing, do not drown; just wash leaves thoroughly and cook.

LEEKS

Leeks are best when picked in early spring. The leaves, when unrolled, are flat and lancehead-shaped. The flavor suggests that of onion with a hint of garlic. When cultivating, pull the entire plant and clean as you would a green onion (removing the outer skin). Eat raw or use for flavoring in cooking.

Lamb's Quarters

MILKWEED (*ASCLEPIAS SYRIACA*)

The milkweed, when picked in early spring, is a whitish-green color. They may grow to a height of 5 feet. The seedbeds grow from 3 to 5 inches long and are covered with soft spines and hair. The stalks emit a milky substance when broken.

Pick stalks and seedbeds; wash thoroughly. Boil for 1 minute; strain, and repeat at least 3 times. Boil once again for 10 minutes. Drain, season and serve.

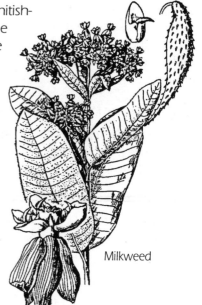

COMMON MORELS

Common morels appear in May. In appearance they resemble long, tiny sponges and have hollow white stems. The cap has irregular pits like that of a honeycomb. To prepare, soak in cold salted water for 2 to 3 hours, before using in any recipe.

Milkweed

STINGING NETTLES (*LAPORTEA CANADENSIS*)

Gather these plants in spring or early summer, wearing gloves, because this plant

releases an irritating oil, rich in formatic acid when
touched. The stinging properties are eliminated
through cooking and drying. Collect the young
top leaves and steam until tender. Serve with
butter. Do not overcook. They need only cook
for about 1 minute. The leaves can also be dried and
used for tea. The stinging nettle suggests the flavor of
spinach.

PUFFBALLS

All puffballs with the flesh are good eating. Avoid
picking the ones that are overripe. These will fall apart
when touched, or if cut open, the center will appear
yellow to greenish-brown. In preparing, if the puffball is
small; simply scrape off the soil, rinse, and wipe with a
damp cloth. Large puffballs should be peeled. The flavor
suggests that of a mushroom.

Stinging Nettles

COMMON PURSLANE (*PORULACA OLERLACEA*)

This plant may be gathered all through the summer
months. In appearance the stems are a reddish color,
the leaves are small and paddle-shaped, and the
flowers are small, 5-petaled and yellow.

When the leaves are used, first wash well and
then they can be used raw in salads or cooked. This is
an excellent substitute for cucumbers.

The seeds can be ground into meal and mixed with
flour to bake breads or boiled and eaten as porridge.

WILD ROSE (*ROSA* FAMILY)

This thorny plant grows in thickets 4 to 6 feet tall
and has oval-shaped, toothed leaves 2 to 4 inches long.
The wild rose is a light-red 5-petaled flower. The fruit can
be eaten raw and suggests the flavor of apples.

AS A SWEETENER: The seeds must be pulverized, boiled
and strained through cheesecloth, to use as a syrup.

AS A TEA: Steep flowers for 5 minutes in boiling water
and sweeten with wild honey.

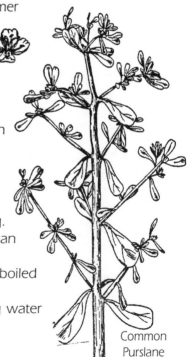

Common
Purslane

WATERCRESS (*NASTURTIUM OFFICINALE*)

This plant should be gathered in the spring and summer. In appearance, the leaves are a shiny, dark green with rounded lobes and the flowers are white and grow in clusters.

Watercress is popular because of its taste, which is superior to any kind of lettuce. In taste it resembles spinach.

To cultivate, snip or pinch off at the water's surface. Do not pull up the entire plant. Wash thoroughly and use in salads or as a fresh or cooked vegetable.

Wild Rose

WOOD SORREL (*OXALIS EUROPEA*)

This plant should be picked in the summer. The flower closely resembles the clover, as the flowers are compounded in 3's and close at night. Flowers range in color from yellow to purple and always have 5 petals. The stems are long and juicy. The wood sorrel has a delicate lemony flavor.

Wash thoroughly and add to soups, stews, or mix in salads.

The stems are full of moisture and make a good thirst-quencher by simply nibbling.

YELLOW PONDLILY (*NUPHAR VARIEGATUM*)

This plant is gathered in the summer and fall, using a canoe or boat. The leaves are large and oval-shaped, with a deep curve at the heart-shaped base. The large & showy flowers are flattened globes made up of half a dozen thick golden sepals arching over the petals. The petals and sepals will rot away, leaving a large fleshy green capsule filled with numerous seeds. Eventually, the pulpy flesh of the fruit disintegrates to release the edible seeds. The taste of the seeds resembles that of the chestnut, and the roots, the taste of a potato.

PREPARATION: Remove outer shell that encloses the seeds;

Wood Sorral

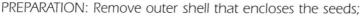

boil seeds to make a gruel, or parch in a hot frying pan until seeds swell and pop open slightly. These cracked seeds can be eaten as is or pounded into meal and used to make bread and porridge. The meal can also be used as a soup thickener. The seeds can be dried and stored in a cool, dark place. The potato-like roots are also delicious edibles. Their overpowering taste can be severed by boiling in two changes of water and seasoned.

CATTAILS

Cattails can grow to a height of 10 feet. They are found in any marshy areas.

CATTAIL SHOOTS: Are easily pulled and have a syrupy core, which is eaten like celery, cooked or raw. The spikes taste similar to corn.

YELLOW POLLEN: When dried and sifted, can be used as flour, either alone or mixed half and half with conventional flour.

ROOTS & ROOTSHOOTS: The boiled sprouts are good with butter or when cooked with meat.

CATTAIL POTATOES: Are found below the shoots and when peeled can be used raw in salads or cooked as potatoes.

Yellow Pond Lily

DANDELIONS

WINE: Flowers should be washed thoroughly and wine preparation begun immediately.

ROOTS: Can be used like chicory for a noncaffeinated coffee substitute.

LEAVES: The cooked leaves suggest the flavor

Dandelion

of spinach. They should be picked before the flowers appear; otherwise they have to be boiled twice to remove the bitterness from them.

FIDDLEHEADS

Fiddleheads get their name from their shape. The best time to cultivate this plant is before it reaches a height of approximately 6 inches, and still appears curled and rusty in color. When picking, pick close to the root.

To prepare, remove rusty colored skin and wash in warm water. Let stand in cold water for 30 minutes.

Serving suggestions: Steam or saute fiddleheads and serve with butter and bacon. The plant suggests the flavor or broccoli or asparagus.

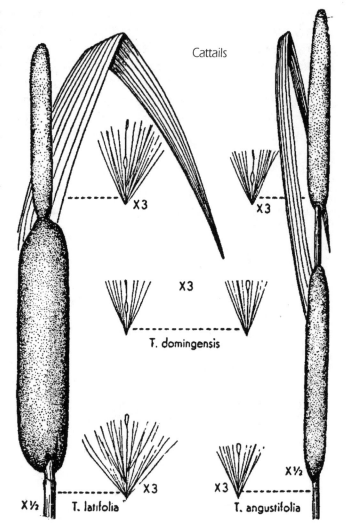

Cattails

X3

X3

X3

T. domingensis

X3

T. latifolia

X3

X½

T. angustifolia

X½

CATTAILS ON THE COB

Cattail spikes

Butter

Water

Gather green cattail spikes in early spring. Clean off in cold water. Place in a pot and cover with water; boil 10 to 15 minutes. When done, drain and serve with butter. Eat like corn on the cob.

CATTAIL PASTRIES

2 cups cattail flour

Vegetable oil

1 tsp. salt

Honey

2 cups water

Scrape and clean several cattail roots. Place on lightly greased cookie sheet in a 200°F oven to dry overnight. Skin roots and remove fibers. Pound roots until a fine flour. Allow to stand overnight to dry. In a saucepan, bring salted water to a boil. Remove from heat and fold in flour. Beat until mixture forms a thick paste. Cool to room temperature. In a deep fryer, heat about 3 inches of oil to a temperature of 400°F or until oil smokes. Spoon out dough onto a floured cookie sheet to form a cake 1/4 inch thick. Cut ribbons 1/2 inch wide and about 5 inches long. Carefully lift ribbons into the hot oil. Deep-fry for 5 minutes or until golden brown, turning at least once. Lift out and set on a paper towel to drain off grease. Serve hot with honey spread on top.

SESHELT CHOWDER

4 big cattail roots, roasted and diced

1 1/2 lbs. roughly cut salmon, fresh

5 cups water

1/4 tsp. fresh pepper

2 tsp. salt

Simmer the cattails roots in the water for 40 minutes. Add remaining ingredients and simmer another 10 minutes.

DANDELION GREENS SUPREME

1 tbsp. margarine
1/4 cup onions, chopped
4 cups chopped dandelion
   greens

2 tbsp. beef broth
2 tbsp. heavy cream
1/4 cup bacon, fried
Salt and pepper to taste

Melt margarine in a deep skillet. Stir in dandelion greens, onions and beef broth. Cover and cook over medium heat for 10 to 12 minutes, stirring occasionally. Mix in heavy cream and bacon. Cook until most of the liquid disappears. Season with salt and pepper.

DANDELION GREENS

4 cups dandelion greens,
   washed
1/2 cup diced onions

2 tbsp. margarine
Salt and pepper to taste

Immerse dandelion greens in boiling salted water. Cook until water returns to a rapid boil. Drain and chop. Saute onions in margarine and mix in greens. Season with salt and pepper.

CREAM OF FIDDLEHEAD SOUP WITH MUSHROOMS

1 lb. fiddleheads
1 can (10 oz.) cream of
   mushroom soup
2 cups milk

1 can (10 oz.) beef consomme
1 tsp. salt
1/2 tsp. pepper

Clean rust and woolly coating from the fiddleheads by rubbing them between the hands and washing under running water. Drop fiddleheads into 1 quart of boiling salted water and boil for 10 minutes. Remove from heat and immerse in cold water for 2 minutes. Drain and set aside. In clean saucepan, bring mushroom soup and milk to a boil over medium heat. Reduce heat to low. Add fiddleheads and cook for 20 minutes. Place a fine sieve over a large bowl and pour hot soup through. With a wooden spoon, rub fiddleheads and mushrooms through as well. Pour mixture from the bowl back into saucepan. Add consomme and simmer over low heat for 5 minutes. Season to taste. If too thick, add a little milk. Garnish with small pieces of fiddleheads and chopped parsley.

MARINATED FIDDLEHEADS

3 cups water
Juice of 1 lemon
5 tbsp. vinegar
1/2 cup oil
1 tsp. salt
2 stalks celery, chopped
1 stalk fennel
2 quarts fiddleheads

In a saucepan combine water, lemon juice, vinegar, oil, salt, celery and fennel. Bring to a boil. Add fiddleheads and simmer 20 minutes, or until fiddleheads are tender. Drain, cool and place in refrigerator until ready to serve.

CLOVER SOUP

2 cups clover flowers and leaves
1 onion, chopped
3 tbsp. butter
2 pints water
3 potatoes, peeled and quartered
Salt and pepper to taste
Parsley
Grated cheddar cheese

Clean and dip clover flowers and leaves in cold salted water. Remove and cut into pieces. In a large saucepan, saute flowers, leaves and onions in butter. When all is softened, add the water, then the potatoes and season with salt and pepper. Cook gently for 20 minutes. Drain the cooking liquid and save it. Puree potato mixture and dilute with the cooking liquid, stirring constantly. Bring to a boil, then reduce heat and simmer for 3 minutes. Garnish with parsley and sprinkle with grated cheese.

HOMEMADE HONEY

10 cups sugar
3 cups water
1/2 tsp. powdered alum
80 white clover blossoms
40 red clover blossoms
Petals from 5 roses (not too
    highly scented)

Boil sugar, water and alum together for 5 minutes. Then pour over blossoms and petals; let stand 20 minutes. Strain through cheesecloth into sterilized containers and seal tightly. The honey can be kept for years.

LAMB'S QUARTERS FRITTERS

1 quart lamb's quarters, washed
1/2 tsp. nutmeg
2 eggs, separated

1/2 cup grated parmesan
   cheese
Oil for deep frying

Boil lamb's quarters for 10 minutes. Strain and then chop. Place in a bowl and sprinkle nutmeg over the leaves. Stir in 2 egg yolks and lastly the parmesan cheese. Allow mixture to cool. Then, beat egg whites and stir into mixture. Drop by spoonfuls into hot oil. Fry until golden brown on both sides. Serve immediately.

LAMB'S QUARTERS AND BACON

5 or 6 strips bacon

2 cups lamb's quarters leaves,
   washed and chopped

Fry bacon until crisp. Remove from frying pan, leaving 2 tablespoons of fat. Add lamb's quarters leaves and fry for about 5 minutes or until leaves are tender. Crumble bacon pieces and mix in with the lamb's quarter leaves. Serve.

GLAZED MILKWEED STALKS

1 dozen young milkweed stalks
1 1/2 cups chicken stock
1/4 cup butter
2 tbsp. sugar

1/2 tsp. salt
1/4 tsp. pepper
2 tbsp. parsley

Clean and peel young milkweed stalks and cut into 2-inch lengths. In a 12-inch skillet, combine chicken stock, butter, sugar, salt, pepper and milkweed stalks. Bring to a boil over moderate heat.

Cover skillet and simmer for about 20 minutes, shaking the pan occasionally to roll the milkweed stalks about in the liquid. When milkweed stalks are tender and the cooking fluid is brown and shiny, the dish is ready to remove from the stove.

Be sure milkweed stalks are well-coated with liquid. Sprinkle with parsley and serve at once.

ALL-FOR-YOU MORELS

1 onion, sliced thin
3 tbsp. butter
2 tbsp. flour
1/4 cup milk

1 lb. morels
Salt and pepper
1 cup sour cream

In a frying pan, saute onion in 2 tablespoons of the butter. In another pan, melt remaining 1 tablespoon of butter and stir in flour. Add milk and stir until smooth. Pour onions into the mixture and add morels. Season with salt and pepper. Then add half of the sour cream, stirring thoroughly, but gently. Cook over medium heat for about 10 minutes; then add remaining sour cream. Heat another 5 minutes and serve.

CORNY MORELS

Morels, as many as gathered
1 small green pepper, sliced thin
Butter

1 tbsp. soy sauce (optional)
1 can corn nibbles

Fry morels and green pepper in melted butter, allowing morels to remain plump. Stir in soy sauce. In a saucepan, heat corn nibbles and then mix in mushrooms and green pepper. Serve.

CREAMED NETTLES

2 cups water
1/2 tsp. salt
2 cups nettle leaves, washed
3 tbsp. butter or margarine
1 tbsp. flour

1/2 cup cream
1 tsp. sugar
Salt and pepper to taste
1/4 tsp. nutmeg
1/4 cup crushed almonds

Bring water and salt to a boil. Add nettle leaves and boil for 2 or 3 minutes. Then, drain and chop. Cook nettles in a saucepan with melted butter for 3 minutes. Stir in flour. Add cream and cook for an additional 5 minutes, until thickened. Stir in sugar and seasonings and sprinkle almonds on top. Serve.

Cow Parsnips were used wherever they could be found. In the Northeast the stalks were peeled and eaten; in the Round Valley, in California, the hollow base of the stem was commonly used as a salt substitute; and the Meskwaki, whose name for it is Skipwa'ok, cooked the roots and ate them like potatoes.

NETTLE SOUP

2 cups nettle leaves
2 tbsp. butter
1 tsp. minced onion

4 cups chicken broth
salt
Sour cream

To pick nettles, wear a pair of gloves and use a pair of shears. Pick enough so that you will have 2 cups of tender top leaves, firmly packed. Pour boiling water over nettles to remove prickles. Drain and chop. Melt butter in saucepan and saute onion for 1 minute. Add broth, nettles, and salt to taste. Simmer a few minutes. Serve topped with a spoonful of sour cream.

PUFFBALLS WITH BACON

1 lb. bacon
Butter or margarine

1 large puffball, sliced thin
Salt and pepper to taste

Cook bacon, drain; set aside, and keep warm. In a skillet, melt a generous amount of butter or margarine over medium heat. Place slices of puffball in skillet and sprinkle with salt and pepper. When slices have browned on one side, turn and brown other side. Serve with bacon.

CREAM PUFFBALLS

3 cups of puffball, diced
1 tbsp. butter
Flour
1/2 cup heavy cream

Salt and pepper to taste
1/4 tsp. nutmeg
Paprika

Saute puffball cubes in butter over low heat. Sprinkle lightly with flour. Then, add cream, salt, pepper and nutmeg. Cover and continue cooking over low heat for 10 to 15 minutes. Garnish with paprika and serve on toast.

PURSLANE GREENS

1/4 cup water
2 cups purslane leaves
2 tbsp. butter or margarine
1/4 cup dry white wine

3 tbsp. lemon juice
1 tbsp. Worcestershire sauce
Salt and pepper to taste

Bring water to a boil and add purslane leaves. Reduce heat and simmer for 5 minutes. Drain and chop. In a heavy frying pan, melt butter and add all the ingredients. Stir gently and heat thoroughly. Serve hot.

PURSLANE AND FRIED EGGS

1/2 cup water
2 cups purslane leaves
1/4 cup butter
1 tsp. white wine vinegar

salt and pepper to taste
2 tbsp. butter
4 eggs

Bring water to a boil and add purslane leaves. Reduce heat and simmer for about 5 minutes. Drain. In a skillet melt the 1/4 cup butter and add purslane leaves, vinegar, salt and pepper. Fry for about 5 minutes over medium heat. In another skillet, melt the 2 tablespoons of butter and fry eggs as desired. When cooked, pour purslane leaves over top and serve.

ROSE FRITTERS

Rose petals, fresh
Brandy
1 egg
3/4 cup flour

1/2 tsp. salt
1/2 cup milk
Powdered sugar

Dip rose petals in brandy, then in a batter made with egg, flour, salt and milk. Fry in deep fat at 375°F for 1 minute. Drain and dust with powdered sugar.

GOLDEN POND LILY STEW

6 green onions, chopped
2 lbs. stewing beef
3 tbsp. butter
12 lily roots, cleaned and sliced
2 cups water

Salt and pepper to taste
1/3 cup dry red wine
2 tbsp. flour, mixed with 1/4
  cup water

In a saucepan, brown onions and stewing beef in melted butter. Add lily roots, water, salt and pepper. Cover and bring to a boil; then reduce heat and simmer for 3 to 4 hours. In the last 15 minutes of cooking time, add wine and stir in flour and water mixture to thicken stew.

ROSE HIP JELLY

4 quarts ripe rose hips
2 quarts water
1/2 cup lemon juice

1 pkg. pectin crystals
5 cups sugar

Simmer rose hips in water until soft. Crush to mash, and strain through a jelly bag. Should make about 4 cups of rose hip juice.

To the juice, add lemon juice and pectin crystals and stir until mixture comes to a hard boil. Stir sugar in at once. Bring to a full rolling boil and boil for 1 minute, stirring constantly.

Remove jelly from heat and skim off foam with metal spoon. Pour into hot sterilized jars.

STEWED WATERCRESS

"The substance of all flesh is the seed of seeds, Corn."
—Zuni saying

1/4 cup butter
1/4 cup flour
1 1/2 cups milk
1/2 cup heavy cream

1/2 tsp. salt
1/2 tsp. white pepper
1 lb. watercress

In a saucepan, melt butter over moderate heat. Remove from heat and stir in flour. Pour in milk and cream stirring constantly. Cook over low heat until the sauce is smooth and thick. Season with salt and pepper. Parboil watercress for about 5 minutes and drain. Then chop very fine. Add to sauce and heat through. Garnish with parsley flakes.

WOOD SORREL SAUCE

2 tbsp. butter
1/4 cup chopped green onions
1/2 cup flour
1 cup beef stock
1 tbsp. sugar

1 tbsp. white vinegar
1/2 cup chopped wood sorrel
   leaves and tubers
1/2 cup heavy cream

In a saucepan, melt butter. When a nutty odor is emitted, add onion and cook until lightly browned. Add flour, stirring constantly until mixture is lightly browned. Add beef stock, sugar and vinegar. Bring to a boil, reduce heat and simmer for 20 minutes or until sauce is smooth. Pour through a sieve. Return sauce to saucepan and add wood sorrel leaves and tubers. Stir in cream and simmer until hot. Serve with beef.

SORREL SOUP

4 cups chicken broth
1/2 cup sorrel leaves

2 egg yolks, well beaten
2 tbsp. sherry

Heat chicken broth and add sorrel. Simmer for 5 minutes. Slowly pour liquid over the beaten egg yolks, whipping briskly to prevent curdling. Return to saucepan and heat but do not boil. Add sherry and serve.

WATER LILY POPCORN

1/2 lb. water lily seeds
2 tbsp. butter

1 1/2 tsp. salt

To separate seeds from floaters, break away green holsters of pods and dump all the seeds into a 4-quart pot of water. Allow to set for 6 to 8 hours, after which seeds will separate from floaters and sink to the bottom of the pot. Skim off surface and drain water through a sieve. Place seeds on a cookie sheet and let dry. If dried in an oven, set at 150°F. If hotter, seeds will pop.

Melt butter in a saucepan, add salt and seeds and cook over high heat as you would popcorn.

"The Tse'-wa-the [Water Chinquapin] with which you feed your children is a sacred food. It is a symbol of life."
—Osage Rite of Vigil

ADOBE BREAD

1 package (1/4 oz.) dry yeast
1/4 cup warm water
2 tablespoons melted lard or
   shortening

1 teaspoon salt
4 1/2 cups flour
1 cup water

Soften the yeast in the warm water in a large mixing bowl. Then mix in the melted lard or shortening and the salt.

Add the flour alternately with the 1 cup water, sifting the flour in a little at a time and beating well after each addition to make a smooth mixture. You will probably have to knead in the final cup of flour.

Shape the dough into a ball, place in a greased bowl, brush lightly with melted lard or shortening, cover with a dry cloth, and set in a warm place to rise for about 1 hour.

When the dough has doubled in bulk, punch it down, turn onto a floured board and knead for about 5 minutes. Divide into two equal parts and shape into two round loaves on a well-oiled board or greased baking tin.

Cover the loaves with a dry cloth, set in a warm place, and let rise for 15 minutes.

Bake the bread in a hot oven, 400°F for 50 minutes or until loaves are lightly browned and sound hollow when thumped. Cool; cut into wedges before serving. Makes 2 loaves.

CACTUS SALAD

1 can (7 1/4 oz.) natural cactus in salt water, drained

1 can (7 oz.) pimento, drained

DRESSING:

3 tbsp. salad oil
2 tbsp. tarragon vinegar
1 scallion, washed and minced

1 clove garlic, peeled and crushed
1/8 tsp. fresh ground pepper

Arrange a bed of cactus on a small platter. Slice the pimento into julienne strips and place over the cactus.

Mix together the dressing ingredients and pour over salad. Marinate in the refrigerator an hour before serving.

During the Civil War, the Pima served as the only Union forces in the Arizona Territory. They successfully engaged and defeated the Confederate forces, keeping the Southern routes to California open.

SQUASH SOUP

1/2 lb. salt pork (sliced)
1 crook neck squash or half a Mother Hubbard squash

10 medium potatoes (quartered)
1 can (#10) whole-kernel corn or 3 cups dried corn

Boil the salt pork in water for 1/2 hour. Then add the other ingredients.

TIMSILAWILD TURNIP SOUP

2 lbs. dry wild turnips
2 lbs. potatoes
1/4 cup flour

1 tsp. salt
Pinch of pepper

Combine ingredients with water in a kettle. Cook until tender.

MOTHER'S VEGETABLE SOUP

3 carrots
1 lb. dried meat or stew meat
4 large potatoes

1 small onion
6 fresh icicle radishes
Salt and pepper seasoning

Dice the carrots. Add the carrots and meat to 3 quarts of water. Boil 1/2 hour. Quarter the potatoes. Dice the onion and radishes. Add to the stew. Boil until soft. Season to taste.

SMOKED SALMON SOUP

1 lb. smoked salmon
4 potatoes, diced
6 cups water

2 tsp. salt
1/8 tsp. pepper
3/4 cup young spinach

Break salmon into bite-sized pieces; add diced potatoes, water, salt and pepper. Bring to boil, reduce heat and cook until potatoes are done (about 20 minutes). Add spinach; simmer 5 minutes longer.

SOUTH RIO CHOWDER

5 cups water
1 tsp. salt
1/4 tsp. pepper
1 cracked shin bone
1 large onion, chopped
1 tbsp. oil

1 medium potato, sliced
3 beets, sliced
3 carrots, sliced
1 cup shredded cabbage
2 summer squash, sliced
2 green chiles, chopped

Bring water, salt, pepper and soup bone to a boil; simmer 45 minutes. Separately saute onion in oil. Add to soup along with remaining ingredients. Simmer until done; remove bone and serve.

BLACK BEAN SOUP

1 cup leeks, sliced
2 cloves garlic, minced
1/3 cup oil

2 lbs. cooked black beans
1/2 cup water
Salt and pepper to taste

Saute leeks and garlic in oil until soft. Mash half the beans in a saucepan. Add sauteed leek-garlic mixture, the water, and salt and pepper. Simmer 40 minutes, stirring occasionally. Stir in remaining beans; heat thoroughly.

WASNA (CORN CAKE)

5 cups parched corn (use white
   flour corn)

3 cups sugar
2 cups tallow or shortening

Grind the corn well. Place in a large mixing bowl. Add the other ingredients, mix well and place the wasna in an oblong pan to serve.

Among the good spirits of the Iroquios are the Three Sisters. They preside over corn beans and squash and are represented as loving each other dearly and dwelling together in peace and unity. In festivals, they are appealed to as, "Our Life."

OYSTER SOUP

2 quarts oysters
2 quarts water
1/2 tsp. salt
2 onions, chopped

1/4 tsp. pepper
2 tbsp. flour
2 tbsp. butter
1 cup cream

Wash oysters and boil in the salted water until they open. Remove oysters and shells. Strain liquid; add onion and pepper, cooking until onion is done. Form flour and butter into a paste; add to broth, stirring until thickened. Add cream and shelled oysters and heat until almost boiling. Serve at once.

Beans which crack open during cooking are sometimes rubbed by Cherokee mothers on the lips of their children in order to make them smiling and good-natured.

PINON SOUP

2 cups chicken broth
1 quart milk
1 lb. pinon nuts
5 scallions, sliced

4 dried mint leaves
1/4 tsp. coriander
1/4 tsp. pepper
Minced chives

Heat all ingredients except chives together until mixture simmers. Simmer for 20 minutes. Puree in blender until smooth. Reheat and garnish with chives. Soup may be served hot or cold.

PINON AND MINT SOUP

6 cups beef consomme
2 cans chick-peas

1/2 cup pinon nuts
2 stalks mint

Combine all ingredients except mint. Bring to a boil and simmer 15 minutes. Turn off heat, add mint, steep 1 minute and serve.

DRIED CORN

12 ears corn

Carefully peel back husks, leaving them attached at base. Clean corn, removing silks. Fold husks back into position. Place on wire rack in large, shallow baking pan, allowing space between ears so air can circulate. Bake at 325°F for 1 1/2 hours. Cool, strip back husks and hang by husks in a dry place until kernels are dry (about a week).

FRUIT ROLLS

Peaches, pears, apricots, or berries may be used. Wash and pit or seed fruit; mash into a puree. Spread on cookie sheets to an even 1/8 to 1/4-inch thickness. Dry in hot sun for 8 to 10 hours or on a shelf in a warm place for 1 to 2 weeks or oven-dry at 150°F for 4 to 5 hours. Dry until puree is firm and edges can be lifted easily. Peel from cookie sheets while still warm and roll into scrolls. Dry in paper or cloth bags for 4 to 5 days and then store in airtight containers.

JUNIPER TEA

20 tender young sprigs of juniper, washed

2 quarts water

Place the juniper sprigs and water in a large saucepan, bring to a boil, cover, reduce heat, and let simmer for 10 minutes. Turn heat off and let tea steep for 10 minutes. Strain and serve.

ZUNIGREEN CHILI STEW

3 lbs. boned lamb, cut into 1 1/2" cubes
Flour
2 tbsp. cooking oil
1/4 tsp. ground black pepper
6 dried juniper berries, crushed
2 onions, peeled and chopped
1 quart water
5 1/2 cups canned hominy (include liquid)

6 green peppers, cored and quartered
2 garlic cloves, peeled and crushed
1 medium red chili pepper, crushed
1 tbsp. salt
2 tsp. oregano
1/2 cup minced parsley

Dust lamb cubes with flour. Brown lamb slowly on all sides in the cooking oil in a large, heavy skillet. As the meat browns, add the black pepper and crushed juniper berries. Transfer meat to paper toweling to drain.

In the same kettle, saute the onions slowly until golden. Return meat to kettle. Mix in the remaining ingredients (except parsley), cover, and simmer for 1 1/2 hours, stirring occasionally. Stir in parsley just before serving.

In the Zuni system of life, the starting point is man, the most finished creature. Man is also the lowest creature because he is the least mysterious and the most dependent on the other animals and living things of the earth.

BEAN MOLD

1/2 lb. dry pea beans
2 strips bacon, diced and
   rendered (reserve drippings)
1/2 cup cornmeal

1 tsp. salt
1/8 tsp. ground pepper
1/2 tsp. paprika
4 dashes Tobasco sauce

Soak beans; cook according to package directions. Drain, reserving 2 cups of the cooking water. If there are not 2 cups, add enough water to complete the measure.

Mash the beans and mix with the bacon drippings, and cornmeal.

Bring the 2 cups of bean cooking water to a boil; add the bean mixture along with the remaining seasonings. Cook until thickened. Pour into a round casserole dish.

BAKED TURNIPS

1 1/2 lbs. small white turnips
1/4 cup melted butter or
   margarine

1/2 tsp. salt
1/4 tsp. coarse ground pepper

Wash turnips well and trim off stems. Parboil for 20 to 30 minutes or until fork will just pierce them.

Place in a shallow baking dish; top with remaining ingredients. Bake at 350°F for 45 minutes.

DRIED CORN SOUP

1 ear dried corn, removed from
   the cob
7 cups water

1 strip (2"x 1") fatback, diced
5 oz. dried beef
1/8 tsp. fresh ground pepper

Soak the corn in 2 cups of the water for 48 hours.

Place the corn and its soaking water in a large saucepan. Add the remaining water and the fatback, and simmer, covered, for about 3 hours and 50 minutes or until the corn is tender but not soft.

Mix in the dried beef and pepper, and simmer, stirring, for 10 minutes more. Serve hot.

EGGS AND WILD ONIONS

5 slices bacon, cut into julienne
    strips
8 eggs, slightly beaten
1 1/2 tsp. salt

1/2 cup minced scallions or
    chives
1 1/2 tbsp. minced parsley
1/2 tsp. fresh ground pepper

Brown the bacon in a large, heavy skillet. Add eggs, salt, scallions, parsley, and pepper, and scramble gently. Serve at once.

FRIED CUCUMBERS

4 large cucumbers, washed and
    cut into 1/8"-thick slices
Salt and coarsely ground pepper
    to taste

Seasoned flour for dusting
Oil or vegetable shortening for
    frying

Spread cucumber slices between layers of paper toweling to dry. Let stand for about an hour. Remove toweling and season slices with salt and pepper.

Dip slices in flour to coat both sides lightly.

Fry quickly in deep fat until slices are golden brown on each side. Drain on paper toweling and serve at once.

HOMINY SOUP

1/4 lb. salt pork, sliced about
    1/4" thick
1 medium onion, peeled and
    sliced thin
2 cans (1 lb. 13 oz. each)
    hominy, drained

1 quart buttermilk
1/2 tsp. salt
1/4 tsp. fresh ground pepper

Render the salt pork thoroughly in a large, heavy kettle. Drain off drippings. Add the onion to the kettle, and saute slowly until golden and transparent.

Mix in hominy and heat gently, stirring, for about 5 minutes. Add buttermilk, salt and pepper, and heat very slowly (do not allow to simmer) for about 5 minutes. This soup should be served warm, not hot.

Tanfula, *made of hominy grits boiled in lye water, was a favorite food among the Choctaw and it was customarily kept ready in every home to serve to visitors.*

BAKED CUCUMBERS

4 cucumbers, peeled and
   quartered lengthwise
2 tbsp. butter or margarine

1 tsp. salt
1/4 tsp. fresh ground pepper
1 tsp. dill seed, crushed

Place a layer of cucumbers in the bottom of an 8"x8"x4" baking dish and dot with half the butter or margarine.

Mix together the seasonings, and sprinkle half over the layer of cucumbers.

Add a second layer of cucumbers, dot with butter, and sprinkle with remaining seasonings.

Bake uncovered in a hot oven, 400°F, for 1 hour. Stir cucumbers lightly once, pushing the top layer to the bottom and lifting the bottom cucumbers to the top. Serve hot.

BEAN CAKE

1/2 lb. pea beans, washed,
   soaked and cooked by pkg.
   directions
1 cup cornmeal
1 cup flour
2 tsp. salt

1 tsp. baking powder
1/8 tsp. fresh ground pepper
1 cup milk
2 eggs, lightly beaten
2 tbsp. cooking oil

Drain the beans thoroughly, and cook to room temperature.

Sift together the cornmeal, flour, salt, baking powder, and pepper. Mix together the milk and eggs, and then stir them into the sifted dry ingredients. Fold in the beans.

Heat the oil in a pan and add to the bean mixture. Place in a cake pan and bake at 350°F for 40 minutes. Serve hot.

ABOUT WILD BERRIES AND NUTS

CRABAPPLE

To be picked in the fall, after the first frost.

WHITE BLOSSOMS: On tree turn to fruit of yellow-green.

HOPA CRAB-APPLE: Pink apple blossoms followed by fruit red all the way through. All recipes use the crabapple differently, so follow directions in recipe being used. Make sure to always wash and remove blossoms and stems. Cut out any bruised or wormy parts.

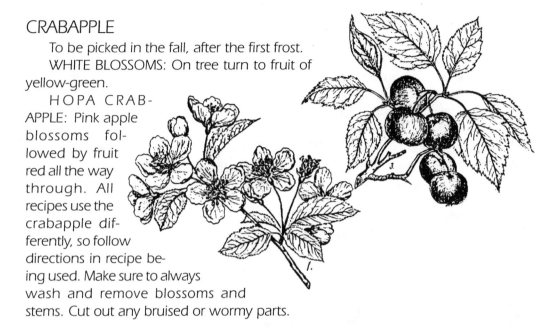

CRANBERRIES

Gather this fruit in October. Cranberries will stay on stem all winter long. The fruit is scarlet red; the stems are trailing and wiry.

There are many ways to use cranberries and they will keep for months and months. Wash well in cold water 2 or 3 times. Pack in sterilized jars and refrigerate. To freeze: lay out on tray and freeze for about 2 hours. When frozen, place in containers or in freezer bags. When needed, rinse in cold water and use in any recipe calling for fresh cranberries.

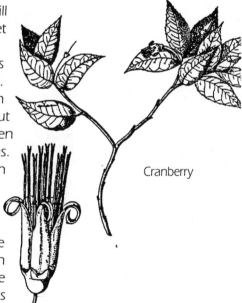

Cranberry

ELDERBERRIES

Pick in July to the middle of August. The berries are magenta-purple, almost black in color, and grow in a single cluster. During June and July, clusters of tiny, creamy-white flowers bloom. These flowers are called "elderblow." Both the berries and the flowers are edible. The Indians used the stems as well. They made maple spiles, pea-shooters, and whistles with them.

The berries are best when dried. Excellent for use in pies, muffins, sauces and juices. Always stew berries with a little sugar first; strain, and use in recipe. Elderberry has little acid and so is best mixed with other fruit.

When using elderblow, simple remove any coarse stems and rinse. Use in favorite recipes.

HUCKLEBERRIES & BLUEBERRIES

HUCKLEBERRY: Is smaller and darker in color than the blueberry and has a hard seedlike berry. Gather these in July and August.

Blueberry

BLUEBERRY: These are gathered in July and August also. The fruits are blue-black in color, with a waxy bloom and many soft seeds.

PREPARATION: Simply pick thorough berries, removing all smashed or green berries. Place in pot filled with water and skim off whatever floats to the top. Use in favorite recipe.

Raspberry

WILD RASPBERRIES

Pick in July or early August. The fruits are red (sometimes yellow) and juicy. Each is an aggregate of several tiny individual fruits. When the berries are ripe, they separate easily from the white central receptacle and fall off in a typical thimble form. Sort through berries carefully, removing any bruised or wormy fruit. Wash in cold water; drain; and let dry. Use in favorite recipes.

STAG SUMAC

EDIBLE BERRIES: Are hard and bright red in color, covered with tiny hairs.

Stag Sumac

POISONOUS BERRIES: Are white in color and hang loosely.

Sumacs are usually found in the same areas as the elderberry. In recipes they complement other, less acidic fruits such as the elderberry.

PREPARATION: Break off fruit in whole clusters, gathering before hard rains wash out most of the acids. Put heads in a large container and cover with water. Using a potato masher, pound and stir for 10 minutes. Always strain juice through a cloth several times to remove any tiny hairs.

Red Oak

ACORNS

Acorns are gathered in the fall. Roasted and salted acorns have a taste that is a cross between sunflower seeds and popcorn.

RED OAKS: Bitter Acorn—Oval-shaped with wooly hairs lining the cup. These acorns will remain on the tree throughout the winter months. To remove the bitterness, first shell; then boil the kernels for 2 hours or more, changing the water each time it becomes tea colored. Use only boiling water for the changes so as not to interrupt the boiling procedure. Continue until water remains clear and nut is chocolate brown in color.

WHITE OAKS: Sweet Acorns—Oval-shaped with smooth inner wall of cup. Needs only to be shelled and roasted.

SUGGESTIONS: Dip dried acorns in clarified sugar; serve. Ground meal can be used as a substitute for conventional flour in baking. Good as a soup thickener. Roasted acorns are also a popular coffee substitute.

BLACK WALNUTS

Gather in the fall. Fruit is globe-shaped and has a fleshly yellow-green husk with a hard black nut inside. Its best to wear gloves when gathering, as shells will discolor your hands. Coloring makes excellent dye, which is almost impossible to remove. The best way to break the husk and shell is with a hammer.

White Oak

BUTTERNUTS

Butternuts should be gathered in the fall. Also referred to as the "white walnut", the butternut fruit is elliptical in shape and the husk is sticky and yellow-green. The kernel is even harder to extract than that of the walnut. You can accomplish this only by repeated blows from a hammer. Use these kernels in place of walnuts. Roast kernels in a moderate oven of about 300°F, until dried. Leave whole, chop or pulverize. Store in glass containers and seal tightly.

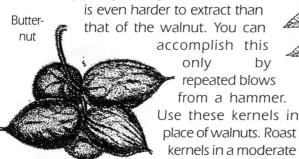

Butter-
nut

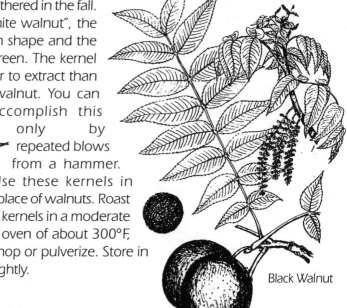

Black Walnut

HAZELNUTS

Pick in the fall after the first frost. Leaves appear alternately on the branches; never in pairs, and are oval shaped and sharply toothed. Nuts have a stinging, tubular husk covering them. To remove skins, spread on baking pan and heat in 325°F oven for 30 minutes; cool. Then skins should rub off easily.

CHESTNUTS

Chestnut trees are very scarce today. The fruit is dark brown with a burred, prickly shell. Found in clusters of 2 to 6 fruit. Roast over open fire for about 10 minutes, then remove from shells. An alternate method is to roast in the oven for about 1 hour on a salted tray; remove from shell and then pour melted butter over the top.

Hazelnut

MAPLE SYRUP

Trees should be tapped early in the spring. Good syrup can be obtained from all maples, but the sugar maple is the most common. To tap the maple tree for sap, make a V-shaped groove through the bark with a knife. Use a spile made from a tin can lid, a piece of birchbark, or elderberry stems, and insert it into the incision to allow the sap to drain. A delicious syrup can be made by boiling the sap for about 2 hours, depending on preferred texture and consistency. An average-sized tree will yield approximately 1 gallon of syrup per year. Two taps or spiles can be put into most trees.

The Indians were the first people to make maple syrup and sugar. A tomahawk was used to make a slant cut into a tree. Then a flat piece of wood was driven into the lower end of the cut. The sap ran along this piece of wood and into a birchbark dish.

Women and girls poured this sap into birchbark pails and carried it to the boiling place. The Indians made boiling kettles of green birchbark because the green bark would not burn for a long time.

During the boiling process, the water evaporates and maple syrup remains. If boiled long enough, the maple syrup will turn into sugar.

Chestnut

SUMAC JELLY

2 quarts crimson sumac heads
Water
3 cups apple juice

1 pkg. pectin crystals
9 cups sugar

Wash sumac, cover with water, and simmer for about 15 minutes. Should make 5 cups of clear crimson sumac juice.

Combine sumac juice, apple juice and pectin crystals and stir until mixture comes to a boil. Then stir in sugar and boil hard for a minute, stirring constantly. Remove from heat and skim off foam. Pour at once into sterilized jars.

RASPBERRY OR BLACKBERRY DUMPLINGS

3 pints raspberries or
   blackberries
3/4 cup water
1 cup sugar
1 1/2 tbsp. margarine

2 cups flour
3 tbsp. sugar
1 tsp. salt
3 1/2 tbsp. baking powder
1 egg
Milk

Combine first 4 ingredients in a saucepan and set aside.

Sift together the flour, 3 tablespoons sugar, salt and baking powder. Add egg and mix well. Stir in enough milk to make a stiff batter. Place saucepan on the heat and bring mixture to a boil. Drop flour mixture in by tablespoonsful. Cover and cook for 15 to 20 minutes. Can be served with ice cream or cream.

SUMACADE

6 to 8 medium-sized sumac fruit
   clusters

6 cups water
1/2 cup·sugar

Wash sumac fruit and break off the main stems of clusters. Place in a large saucepan with the water and bruise fruit thoroughly until water turns pink. Remove larger pieces and strain as you would to make jelly. Add sugar and stir until dissolved. Serve cold as is or mix it half and half with other fruit juices.

WILD APPLESAUCE

4 lbs. wild crab apples (cored but not peeled) cut in slices

8 oz. (1/2 pound) maple sugar
4 cups water

Place all ingredients together in a large saucepan. Bring to a boil and reduce heat. Simmer 50 minutes, stirring frequently.

TRADITIONAL CRANBERRY SAUCE

1 1/2 lbs. wild high bush cranberries or domestic cranberries

2 cups maple sugar
1 1/2 cups birch sap or spring water

Place all ingredients in a large saucepan and bring to a boil. Reduce heat and simmer 25 to 30 minutes. Cool and serve with wild meat.

WILD CRANBERRY CONSERVE

1 quart cranberries
1 1/2 cups water
1 1/2 lbs. sugar

1 lb. raisins
1 large orange, sliced

Wash and pick over cranberries, then cook them in water until they have burst. Add all remaining ingredients and cook for 25 minutes. Stir often. Place in small sterilized jars and seal.

WILD CRANBERRY JUICE

2 cups cranberries
3 cups water

1/2 cup sugar
1/2 cup apple juice
2 tbsp. lemon juice

Cook cranberries in water for 5 minutes. Strain through cheesecloth. Boil juice and add sugar, stirring until sugar is dissolved, about 2 minutes. Add apple and lemon juices and chill.

WILD CRANBERRY SAUCE

4 cups cranberries
2 cups water

2 cups sugar

Wash and pick over cranberries; cook them in the water until berries burst. Strain, rubbing as much as possible of the pulp through a sieve. Add sugar and stir until dissolved. Boil rapidly for 12 to 15 minutes. Chill.

ELDERBERRY CATSUP

2 quarts elderberries
Vinegar to cover
1 cup sugar
1 tsp. cinnamon

1 tbsp. allspice
1 tbsp. cloves
1/4 tsp. cayenne pepper

Cook elderberries in vinegar until berries burst. Put berries through a food press or sieve; add sugar, cinnamon, allspice, cloves and cayenne. Simmer until thickened. Pour into sterilized jars and seal.

ELDERFLOWER FRITTERS

2 eggs, well beaten
1/2 cup flour
3/4 tsp. salt
1/4 tsp. pepper
1 tsp. melted butter

1 tbsp. brandy
Elderflowers, washed and
    drained
Fat for deep frying
Powdered sugar

Combine eggs, flour, salt, pepper, butter and brandy together. Beat well. Dip flowers in batter and fry in deep fat at 350°F until crisp and brown. Drain on paper towels. Sprinkle with powdered sugar and serve hot.

CURRIED FRUIT WITH WILD BLUEBERRIES

1 cup wild blueberries
1 cup raspberries
1 cup diced pears
1 cup diced peaches

1/3 cup melted butter
3 tsp. curry powder
3/4 cup brown sugar

Place fruit into a shallow baking dish. Combine butter, curry powder and brown sugar together. Pour over fruit. Marinate overnight. Bake at 350°F for 1 hour.

WILD BLUEBERRY COOKIES

2 cups flour
2 tsp. baking powder
1/2 tsp. salt
3/4 cup wild blueberries

1/2 cup shortening
1 cup sugar
1 1/2 tsp. grated lemon rind
1 egg
1/4 cup milk

Combine flour, baking powder and salt; stir in blueberries. In a separate bowl cream shortening until soft; gradually beat in sugar, then lemon rind and egg. Add flour mixture alternately with milk, beating until smooth after each addition. Drop from teaspoon onto greased cookie sheet. Bake at 375°F for 8 to 12 minutes.

WILD BLUEBERRY PANCAKES

1 1/2 cups all-purpose flour
1 1/2 cups whole wheat flour
2 tsp. baking powder
2 tsp. baking soda
1/2 cup granulated sugar

1 1/2 tsp. salt
3 eggs
1/2 cup melted margarine
1 cup plain yogurt
1 cup milk
2 cups wild blueberries

Combine all dry ingredients in a large bowl. In a separate bowl, beat together eggs, margarine, yogurt and milk.

Make a well in center of dry ingredients and stir in egg mixture until blended but still lumpy.

Spoon 1/4 cup of batter onto an oiled, hot skillet and sprinkle with a few blueberries. When bubbles form and hold in batter, flip and cook until bottom is browned.

Serve with butter and maple syrup.

During the strawberry season, the Iroquois held a festival. The women would gather the berries from the field and when they returned the great feather dance would begin; after the dancing was done, children would be given baskets containing berries mixed with water and maple sugar which they presented to each person in the village, who would then give thanks as they received it.

HUCKLEBERRY MUFFINS

1 cup huckleberries
1/2 cup brown sugar
2 cups all-purpose flour
1 tbsp. baking powder
1/2 tsp. salt

2 eggs
1/4 cup milk
1 tsp. vanilla
1/4 cup melted margarine
1/4 cup syrup

Combine huckleberries and sugar. Stir in flour, baking powder and salt. In a separate bowl, beat together eggs, milk, vanilla, margarine and syrup. Combine the two mixtures, using a fork to stir. Do not overmix. Fill well-greased muffin tins, three quarters full. Bake at 450°F for 20 to 25 minutes.

WILD RASPBERRY CAKE

1 3/4 cups flour
1/2 tsp. salt
1 cup white sugar
1 tsp. cinnamon
3/4 cup shortening

1 tsp. Baking soda (dissolved in
   1/2 cup milk)
2 eggs, slightly beaten
1 cup raspberries

Sift together flour, salt, sugar and cinnamon. Cut in shortening. Then mix in soda mixture, eggs and raspberries. Pour into a greased pan and bake at 325°F for 1 hour.

BLUEBERRY-ORANGE LOAF

2 cups all-purpose flour
3/4 cup sugar
2 tsp. baking powder
1/2 tsp. baking soda
3/4 tsp. salt
1 egg, beaten

3/4 cup milk
1/4 cup orange juice
1/4 cup melted butter
1 tbsp. grated orange rind
1 cup blueberries
1/2 cup chopped nuts

Sift together first 5 ingredients into a bowl. In a separate bowl combine the next five ingredients; stir into flour mixture. Beat well. Grease a 9x4x3-inch loaf pan and spread with 1/3 of the batter. Sprinkle on 1/2 the blueberries and nuts. Add 1/3 more batter; then the remaining blueberries and nuts. Add rest of batter. Bake at 350°F for 50 minutes. Add frosting if desired when cool.

WILD RASPBERRY BREAD PUDDING

2 cups sugar
10 cups wild raspberries,
    cleaned and dried

12 slices homemade white
    bread
2 cups heavy cream

In a large bowl, sprinkle sugar over raspberries. Toss berries very lightly until all sugar has dissolved. Cover and set aside. Cut slice of bread to fit the bottom of a deep 2-quart bowl.

Trim 8 or 9 slices of bread into wedges about 4 inches at the top and 3 inches across bottom. Line sides of bowl with wedges, overlapping each one by about 1/2 inch.

Pour fruit into the bowl and cover top completely with the rest of the bread. Cover top of bowl with a flat plate and place a weight on top of plate. Place in refrigerator for at least 12 hours.

Remove mold by quickly inverting it onto a chilled serving plate. The mold should slide out easily. Whip cream in a large chilled bowl until it holds its shape. With a spatula, cover pudding mold on the outside and top with whipped cream. Serve chilled.

HUCKLEBERRY CRISP

1/3 cup sugar
2 tbsp. cornstarch
1/4 tsp. salt
1/4 tsp. cinnamon
1/4 tsp. nutmeg

1 tbsp. lemon juice
4 cups huckleberries, sweetened
1 cup huckleberry juice (drained
    from fruit)

Combine sugar, cornstarch, salt and spices in a saucepan. Add lemon and huckleberry juices and stir until smooth.

Cook over low heat until thickened and clear, stirring constantly. Stir in huckleberries and pour into a greased baking dish.

Prepare Topping. Sprinkle over the huckleberry mixture and bake at 400°F for 30 minutes or until topping is crisp and golden brown. Serve warm or cold.

TOPPING:

1/3 cup butter or margarine
1 cup brown sugar, firmly
    packed

2 tbsp. flour
3 cups cornflakes

Melt butter in a saucepan. Combine sugar and flour and add to butter. Cook, stirring constantly, over low heat for 3 minutes. Add cornflakes, mixing quickly until they are coated with syrup.

BLUEBERRY CAKE

1/2 cup butter or margarine
1 cup + 1 tbsp. white sugar
1/4 tsp. salt
1 tsp. vanilla
2 eggs, separated

1 1/2 cups + 1 tbsp. flour
1 tsp. baking powder
1/3 cup milk
1 1/2 cups blueberries

Cream butter and 3/4 cup of the sugar. Add salt and vanilla. Add egg yolks. Beat until creamy. Combine 1 1/2 cups of the flour and the baking powder. Add alternately with milk to egg mixture. Beat egg whites until soft, adding 1/4 cup of the remaining sugar. Beat until stiff. Coat berries with remaining 1 tbsp. flour and add to batter. Fold in egg whites. Pour into greased 8-inch cake pan. Sprinkle remaining 1 tbsp. sugar on top. Bake at 350 °F for 50 minutes, or until toothpick inserted into the center of cake comes out clean.

BAKED RHUBARB AND STRAWBERRIES

1/2 lb. rhubarb
1/2 lb. strawberries

1 cup brown sugar

Wash rhubarb; cut in 2-inch cubes. Add strawberries and sugar, mix with rhubarb. Place mixture in baking dish, and cover and bake at 350°F for 35 to 45 minutes.

STRAWBERRIES AND HONEY SAUCE

6 oz. cream cheese
1/2 cup honey

1 cup sour cream
2 tbsp. white wine

Combine cheese, honey and sour cream until perfectly smooth. Stir in wine. Place strawberries on a serving dish and spoon honey sauce over them.

SIMMERED GOOSEBERRIES

1 quart gooseberries   1 1/2 cups water
1 1/2 cups sugar

Wash berries and remove the blossoms. Pick off stems and remove any berries that are soft. Put sugar and water in a saucepan and bring to a boil. Then add berries and simmer till berries are cooked through, stirring occasionally. Do not let berries get soft and mushy.

PUMPKIN SOUP

1 can (1 lb. 13 oz.) water-packed   1/2 tsp. powdered marjoram
    pumpkin puree   Dash fresh ground pepper
1 quart milk   1/4 tsp. cinnamon
2 tbsp. butter or margarine   1/4 tsp. mace
4 tbsp. honey   1 tsp. salt
2 tbsp. maple syrup or light   Juice of 1 orange
    brown sugar

Heat pumpkin puree, milk, butter and honey together slowly in a large saucepan, stirring. Combine maple syrup, marjoram, pepper, cinnamon, mace and salt; stir into pumpkin-milk mixture. Heat slowly, stirring to simmering point. Do not boil. Add the orange juice, a little at a time, stirring constantly. Serve hot.

CHERRY BALLS

1 lb. dried chokecherries   1 cup sugar
1 cup tallow or shortening

Grind up wild chokecherries. Add tallow or shortening; then add the sugar. Form into balls the size of a golf ball. This was always a treat for the Sioux children. You may substitute pounded dried beef or venison in place of the chokecherries.

PLAINS INDIAN DESSERT

Bring whole wild chokecherries to a boil just covering them with water. Mash gently with potato masher. Strain juice from chokecherries into a pan; add 1 cup sugar for each pint of juice and 2 tablespoons of cornstarch.

Heat and stir until thickness of custard. Serve in individual bowls, either warm or cold. Plums or other wild fruit may be used instead of chokecherries.

CHERRY WOZAPI (DESSERT)

6 patties of dried cherries (soaked for 1 hour until soft)
1/2 cup flour

Bits of tallow for flavoring
1 cup sugar

Boil the cherry patties in water for 2 hours. Drain the liquid and use for the sauce. Mix the white sauce and gradually add to the cherry liquid. Stir carefully. Add the tallow and sugar. Stir well until it reaches a thick consistency, when it is ready to serve.

The maple was not only a source of sugar. The sap wood was dried and pounded to use in bread and, among the Calmucks, the large seeds were boiled and eaten after they removed the "wings."

ACORN MEAL

Make meal by grinding dry, raw acorn kernels. Mix with boiling water and press out liquid through a cheesecloth. With very bitter acorns, repeat this process several times. Then spread meal on a tray and thoroughly dry in oven at 250°F.

This meal will cake during the drying process. Re-grind using a food chopper. Then, seal in containers, preferably glass jars.

ACORN BREAD

1 cup acorn meal
1 cup white flour
2 tbsp. baking powder
1/2 tsp. salt

3 tbsp. sugar
1 egg, beaten
1 cup milk
3 tbsp. oil

Sift together acorn meal, flour, baking powder, salt and sugar. In separate bowl, mix together egg, milk and oil. Combine dry ingredients and liquid ingredients. Stir just enough to moisten dry ingredients. Pour into a greased pan and bake at 400°F for 30 minutes.

ACORN PANCAKES

1 cup acorn meal
1 cup white flour
2 tbsp. baking powder
1 tsp. salt

3 tbsp. sugar
2 eggs, beaten
1 1/2 cups milk
3 tbsp. oil

Sift together dry ingredients. In separate bowl mix together eggs, milk and oil. Then, combine dry ingredients with liquid mixture. Spread batter thinly on a hot griddle. When edges begin to bubble, flip and brown on other side. Serve with maple syrup or jelly.

BUTTERNUT SAUCE

2 tsp. parsley
1 tsp. tarragon
2 cups butternuts, shelled

1/2 cup olive oil
Salt and pepper to taste
Juice of 1/2 lemon

Blend parsley, tarragon and butternuts in a blender. Add olive oil, seasonings and lemon juice. Blend thoroughly on medium speed. This sauce is a nice dip for cold fish.

MAPLE NUTS

8 oz. grated maple sugar
6 oz. water
3 oz. walnuts or acorns

14 oz. dried prunes (stoned)
4 oz. broken wild hazelnuts

Place maple sugar and water in a large saucepan. Heat slowly without stirring. Remove from heat, drop walnuts in this hot syrup and stir to be sure all parts are sugared. Then drop in, alternately, hazelnuts and prunes and stir well. Remove with a skimming ladle and cool.

When the maple trees were tapped by the Iroquois in early spring, the war dance would be performed to bring warmer weather that would allow the sap to flow. As a special favor to some parents, the dancing warriors would often carry infant boys in their arms while they performed; it was thought that this would inspire the child to lead the life of a warrior.

BLACK WALNUT SOUFFLE

1/4 lb. butter
6 eggs, separated
1/2 cup cream

1/2 cup sugar
1 cup walnuts or butternuts,
    finely chopped

In a bowl, cream butter. Add egg yolks, one at a time, beating between each addition. Then, add cream, sugar and nuts, beating continuously. Whip egg whites stiff and fold them into the creamy mixture. Then pour into a greased souffle dish and bake at 375°F for 1 hour.

BUTTERNUT CAKE

2 cups flour
1 tsp. baking soda
2 tsp. cream of tartar
1 1/2 cups sugar

1/2 melted cup butter
3 eggs, beaten
1/2 cup milk

FILLING:

1 cup sweet cream
1 tbsp. cornstarch, mixed with 2
    tbsp. cold milk

1 tbsp. sugar
2 cups butternuts, pulverized

Combine flour, soda, cream of tartar and sugar. Mix in butter, eggs and milk. Grease 2 (8 inch) round pans and pour the batter in. Bake at 350°F for 35 to 45 minutes.

To make filling, let cream come to a boil, then stir in cornstarch mixture and sugar. Bring to a boil again and remove from stove. Stir in the butternuts. When partially cooled, spread between the 2 layers.

CHESTNUT SOUP

2 celery stalks and leaves
1 tsp. parsley
1 tsp. thyme
1 lb. prepared chestnuts

Salt and pepper to taste
2 cups chicken broth
1/2 cup cream
1 tbsp. sherry
Whipped cream

Tie celery, parsley, and thyme together in a cheesecloth bag. In a soup kettle combine chestnuts, herbs and seasonings and cover with boiling water. Simmer until chestnuts are soft. Remove herbs and either sieve the soup or put it into a blender. Add chicken broth and cream and bring to a boil. Add sherry and serve at once with salted whipped cream.

CHESTNUTS AND BACON

12 chestnuts   12 strips of bacon

Remove shells and skins of the chestnuts. Cover with boiling water and simmer until tender. Drain. Fasten bacon strips around chestnuts with toothpicks. Put under boiler until bacon is crisp.

HAZELNUT CAKES

2 cups hazelnuts, unroasted   1/3 cup cornmeal
2 cups water   1 tsp. salt
                                1/4 cup vegetable oil

Grind nuts and mix with the water in a saucepan. Heat to boiling; reduce heat and simmer for 30 minutes, stirring frequently. Mix in cornmeal and salt and let stand for 20 minutes or until it thickens. Drop large spoon of the nut batter on greased grill. When browned on one side flip cakes over and brown the other side. Serve with butter and honey or maple syrup.

SPICED CRABAPPLES

Crabapples   1 tbsp. stick cinnamon
1 quart vinegar   1 tbsp. whole cloves
4 cups sugar   1 tbsp. mace
                                1 tbsp. allspice

Wash and remove blossom end of firm crabapples. Do not peel. Mix vinegar, sugar and spices. Boil until syrup coats a spoon. Add apples, reheat mixture slowly to avoid bursting the skins. Simmer until apples are tender. Pack into hot, sterile jars. Cover with hot syrup and seal.

To save time and work, the Dakota Sioux would raid the burrows of voles, which collected large amounts of hog peanuts and stored them. However, when the Sioux took the peanuts they always replaced them with an equal quantity of corn or seeds so that the voles would not starve through the winter.

✳ CHAPTER NINE ✳
HERBAL REMEDIES AND HOMEMADE WINES

HERBAL AND NATURAL REMEDIES

Natural medicines are made from many of the trees and their bark, plants and berries found around your home, near campsites, along the roads and in the woods. These are not magic medicines, and all should be investigated by you, your doctor, and the government before you use any homemade remedies. Then and only then should you try them, but remember, people are individuals and these remedies may affect you differently. Use at your own risk. We will include a large selection of these in our next book.

Here are three common wild-plant cures.

FOR EXTERNAL SWELLING:

Pulverize the fresh *Pipsisswea* plant and apply moist to the swelling.

FOR SORE THROAT:

Toast *Juniper twigs* and make a hot pack out of a piece of leather. Place it on the throat.

TOOTHACHE:

Crush the bark of the *Butternut tree* and apply to the sore tooth.

BEETROOT WINE

6 lbs. beets
1 gallon water
2 lbs. seedless raisins
Juice of 2 lemons

Few grains of rice
3 lbs. white sugar
1 oz. yeast
1 slice toast

Wash beets and cut into small pieces. Boil gently in the 1 gallon water for 2 hours. Strain and pour into a large crock. Add raisins, lemon juice, and rice; then stir in sugar until completely dissolved.

Spread yeast on one side of the toast and place toast yeast-side down, on the liquid. Cover and let stand 10 to 12 days, stirring three times daily. Strain and bottle.

WILD RICE WINE

3 lbs. wild rice, cleaned
3 lbs. sugar
1 gallon warm water
1 lb. raisins, ground or chopped
    fine

1 lemon
1 oz. cherry wine yeast
Pinch of isinglass (clearing
    agent)

Put the rice and sugar in a large bowl and cover with the warm water. Mix in raisins. Squeeze the juice from the lemon and add to the mixture. Make sure the temperature of the water is not over 65°F; then sprinkle the yeast and isinglass over the top. Cover and allow to ferment for nine days, stirring frequently for the first three days. After nine days, strain through a paper-filtered, fine sieve.

Transfer the liquid into gallon fermenting jars. Put on the fermentation locks and let stand. When the wine is completely clear, bottle and store. The wine is harsh and strong, but the taste improves greatly with age.

DANDELION WINE

4 quarts dandelion blossoms
4 quarts water
3 lbs. sugar

3 lemons, sliced
1 yeast cake

Combine blossoms and water in a crock and let stand, covered, for nine days. Squeeze out the blossoms and strain juice. Add sugar, lemons and yeast cake and let stand for another nine days.

Strain liquid and put it in a jug, leaving the cork out until fermentation ceases. Then cork it!

The use of Sassafras in making tea and gumbo file was learned from the Choctaw, who gathered the young leaves and roots in the spring and dried them to last throughout the year.

✳ CHAPTER TEN ✳
SMOKING AND CURING
OF FISH AND GAME

Lacking refrigeration, Native Indians developed many ways of preserving foods. Meat and seafood were smoked or dried; vegetables and fruits were dried. Often caches of preserved food were stored in trees under cedar bark so hunters did not have to carry large supplies of food with them on their travels. The Blackfeet also pickled their meat in brine in a process similar to modern corned beef.

Fruits and vegetable were commonly sun-dried. In the damper climates, such as that of the Northwest, some tribes used drying racks of woven cedar mats placed over open fires. Fruits and berries were mashed into a pulp and spread thinly over sheets to make fruit leathers or dried in brick form. Combinations of various fruits and berries in season produced delicious flavor variations.

Dried meat and fruits were rehydrated for use in the winter. You may find this interesting to try; the flavor is different from the same recipe make with fresh ingredients.

Cold-smoked meat keeps much longer than cooked smoking where the temperatures are higher, 150-200°F. Indians cold-smoked meat by hanging it high over the cooking fire for about a week.

For smoking game meat the best woods are mesquite, hickory, oak and citrus. Fish taste best when cooked over a buttonwood, mangrove or baywood fire.

In addition to the recipes that follow; please see the following recipes and pages:

CURED VENISON

3 lbs. salt   1/4 cup cinnamon
5 tbsp. pepper   1/4 cup allspice

Cut meat into strips 12 inches long, 2 inches thick and 4 inches wide. Remove all membranes so curing mixture will adhere to moist meat. Mix dry ingredients thoroughly and rub well into every surface of meat; dust on extra as well. Thread each strip on a string and hang in a cool, dry place out of sun and artificial heat. Meat needs to be hung for approximately a month before eating.

SMOKED HERRING

1 lb. coarse salt   2 cups brown sugar
1 tbsp. salt, pepper   2 tbsp. minced garlic
1 tbsp. cloves, crushed   1 tbsp. bay leaves, crushed
2 tbsp. minced onions   2 lbs. herring

Make a paste of all ingredients except herring. Clean and gut herring. Coat herring with paste and cure for seven days in refrigerator. Reapply mixture as needed so fish remains coated. After seven days, rinse and hang thoroughly to dry. Cold-smoke over fire. For home smokers, smoke at 70-85°F for seven days.

SMOKE-CURED EGGS

Remove the egg sack from salmon, making sure not to put any holes in it. Tie ends with string and hang at the side of the fire. Smoke from the fire will dry and cure it in about four days. When done, it is firm and dry inside and out. It looks and tastes like sausage.

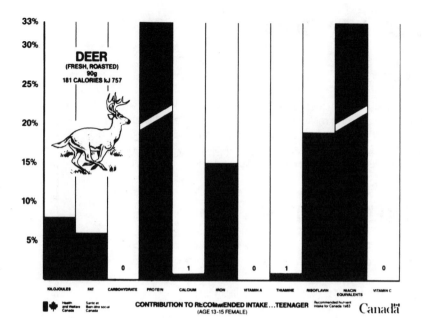

DEER
(FRESH, ROASTED)
90g
181 CALORIES kJ 757

33%
30%
25%
20%
15%
10%
5%

KILOJOULES	FAT	CARBOHYDRATE	PROTEIN	CALCIUM	IRON	VITAMIN A	THIAMINE	RIBOFLAVIN	NIACIN EQUIVALENTS	VITAMIN C
		0		1		0	1			0

Health and Welfare Canada · Santé et Bien-être social Canada

CONTRIBUTION TO RECOMMENDED INTAKE...TEENAGER
(AGE 13-15 FEMALE)

Recommended Nutrient Intake for Canada 1983

Canadä

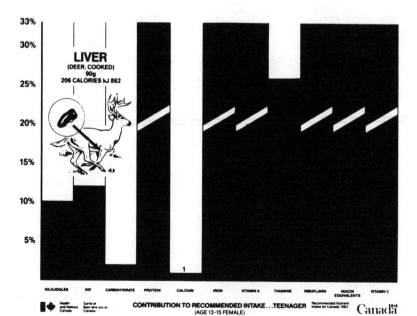

LIVER
(DEER, COOKED)
90g
206 CALORIES kJ 862

33%
30%
25%
20%
15%
10%
5%

KILOJOULES	FAT	CARBOHYDRATE	PROTEIN	CALCIUM	IRON	VITAMIN A	THIAMINE	RIBOFLAVIN	NIACIN EQUIVALENTS	VITAMIN C
				1						

Health and Welfare Canada · Santé et Bien-être social Canada

CONTRIBUTION TO RECOMMENDED INTAKE...TEENAGER
(AGE 13-15 FEMALE)

Recommended Nutrient Intake for Canada 1983

Canadä

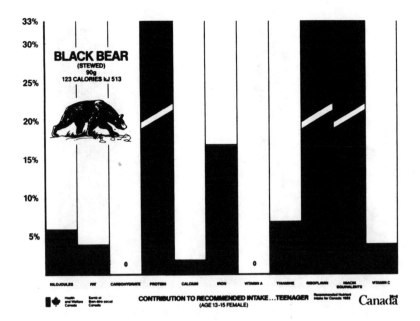

BLACK BEAR
(STEWED)
90g
123 CALORIES kJ 513

33%
30%
25%
20%
15%
10%
5%
0

KILOJOULES | FAT | CARBOHYDRATE | PROTEIN | CALCIUM | IRON | VITAMIN A | THIAMINE | RIBOFLAVIN | NIACIN EQUIVALENTS | VITAMIN C

Health and Welfare Canada · Santé et Bien-être social Canada

CONTRIBUTION TO RECOMMENDED INTAKE...TEENAGER
(AGE 13-15 FEMALE)

Recommended Nutrient Intake for Canada 1983

Canada

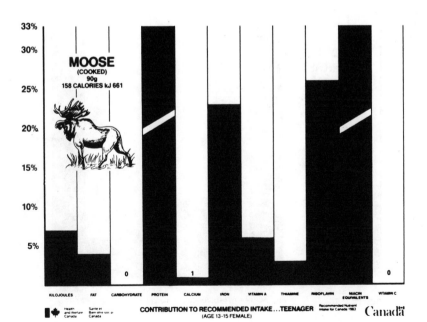

MOOSE
(COOKED)
90g
158 CALORIES kJ 661

33%
30%
25%
20%
15%
10%
5%
0

KILOJOULES | FAT | CARBOHYDRATE | PROTEIN | CALCIUM | IRON | VITAMIN A | THIAMINE | RIBOFLAVIN | NIACIN EQUIVALENTS | VITAMIN C

Health and Welfare Canada · Santé et Bien-être social Canada

CONTRIBUTION TO RECOMMENDED INTAKE...TEENAGER
(AGE 13-15 FEMALE)

Recommended Nutrient Intake for Canada 1983

Canada

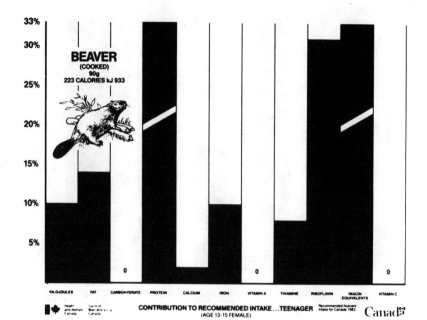

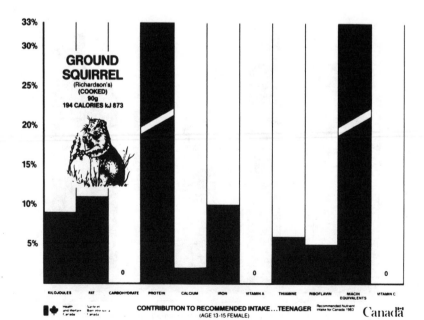

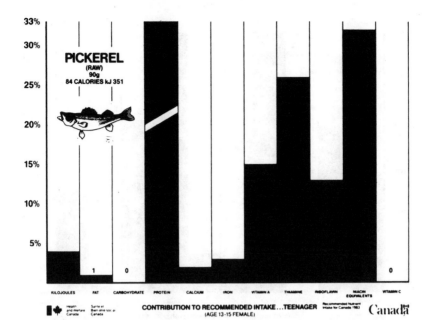

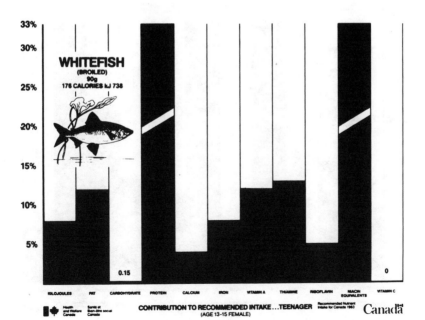

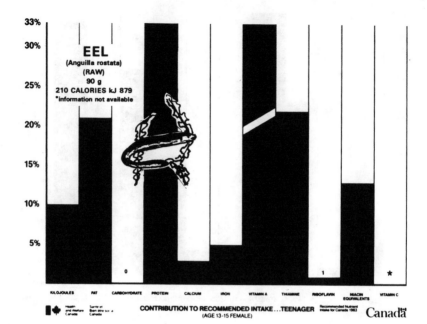

EEL
(Anguilla rostata)
(RAW)
90 g
210 CALORIES kJ 879
*information not available

| 33% |
| 30% |
| 25% |
| 20% |
| 15% |
| 10% |
| 5% |

0   1   *

KILOJOULES FAT CARBOHYDRATE PROTEIN CALCIUM IRON VITAMIN A THIAMINE RIBOFLAVIN NIACIN EQUIVALENTS VITAMIN C

Health and Welfare Canada   Santé et Bien-être social Canada   **CONTRIBUTION TO RECOMMENDED INTAKE...TEENAGER**   Recommended Nutrient Intake for Canada 1983   Canada
(AGE 13-15 FEMALE)

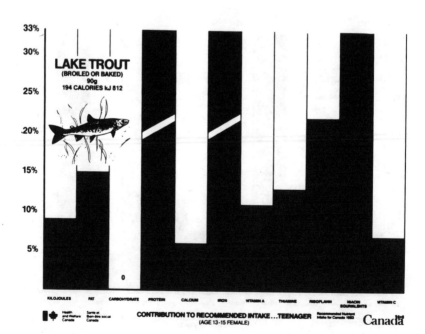

LAKE TROUT
(BROILED OR BAKED)
90g
194 CALORIES kJ 812

| 33% |
| 30% |
| 25% |
| 20% |
| 15% |
| 10% |
| 5% |

0

KILOJOULES FAT CARBOHYDRATE PROTEIN CALCIUM IRON VITAMIN A THIAMINE RIBOFLAVIN NIACIN EQUIVALENTS VITAMIN C

Health and Welfare Canada   Santé et Bien-être social Canada   **CONTRIBUTION TO RECOMMENDED INTAKE...TEENAGER**   Recommended Nutrient Intake for Canada 1983   Canada
(AGE 13-15 FEMALE)

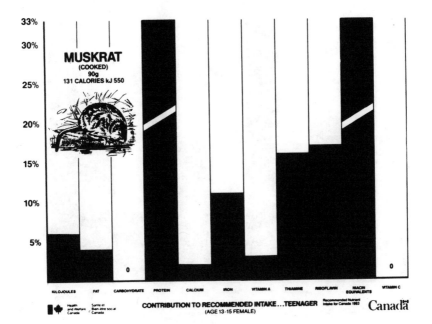

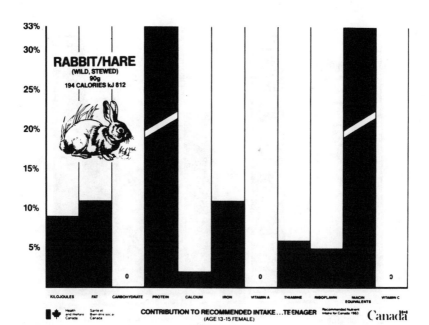

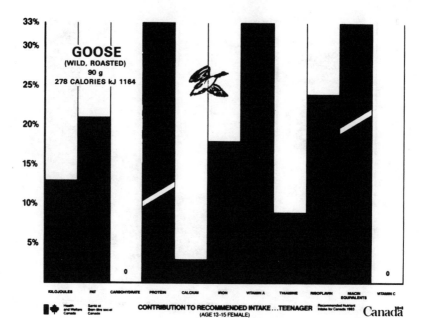

GOOSE
(WILD, ROASTED)
90 g
278 CALORIES kJ 1164

KILOJOULES FAT CARBOHYDRATE PROTEIN CALCIUM IRON VITAMIN A THIAMINE RIBOFLAVIN NIACIN EQUIVALENTS VITAMIN C

Health and Welfare Canada Santé et Bien-être social Canada
CONTRIBUTION TO RECOMMENDED INTAKE...TEENAGER
(AGE 13-15 FEMALE)
Recommended Nutrient Intake for Canada 1983
Canada

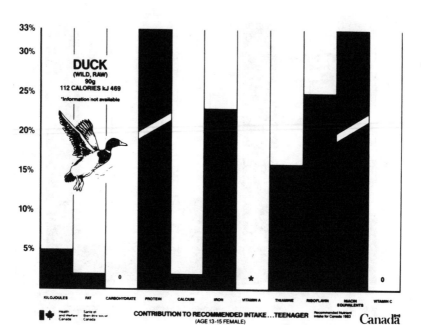

DUCK
(WILD, RAW)
90g
112 CALORIES kJ 469
*Information not available

KILOJOULES FAT CARBOHYDRATE PROTEIN CALCIUM IRON VITAMIN A THIAMINE RIBOFLAVIN NIACIN EQUIVALENTS VITAMIN C

Health and Welfare Canada Santé et Bien-être social Canada
CONTRIBUTION TO RECOMMENDED INTAKE...TEENAGER
(AGE 13-15 FEMALE)
Recommended Nutrient Intake for Canada 1983
Canada

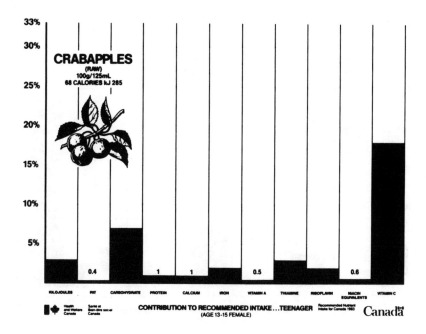

CRABAPPLES
(RAW)
100g/125mL
68 CALORIES kJ 285

33%

30%

25%

20%

15%

10%

5%

| KILOJOULES | FAT | CARBOHYDRATE | PROTEIN | CALCIUM | IRON | VITAMIN A | THIAMINE | RIBOFLAVIN | NIACIN EQUIVALENTS | VITAMIN C |

0.4   1   1   0.5   0.6

CONTRIBUTION TO RECOMMENDED INTAKE...TEENAGER
(AGE 13-15 FEMALE)

Health and Welfare Canada   Santé et Bien-être social Canada   Recommended Nutrient Intake for Canada 1983   Canada

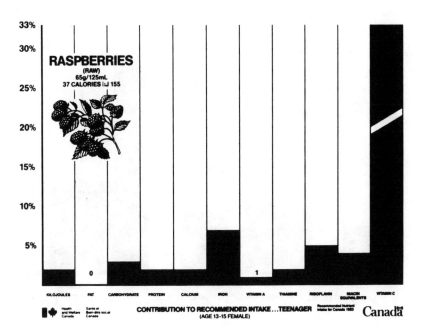

RASPBERRIES
(RAW)
65g/125mL
37 CALORIES kJ 155

33%

30%

25%

20%

15%

10%

5%

| KILOJOULES | FAT | CARBOHYDRATE | PROTEIN | CALCIUM | IRON | VITAMIN A | THIAMINE | RIBOFLAVIN | NIACIN EQUIVALENTS | VITAMIN C |

0   1

CONTRIBUTION TO RECOMMENDED INTAKE...TEENAGER
(AGE 13-15 FEMALE)

Health and Welfare Canada   Santé et Bien-être social Canada   Recommended Nutrient Intake for Canada 1983   Canada

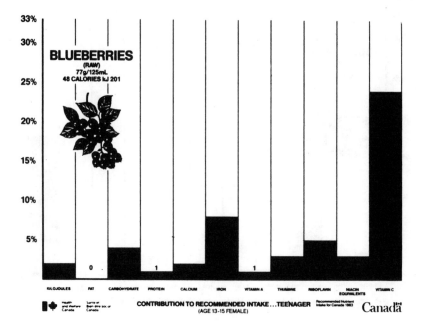

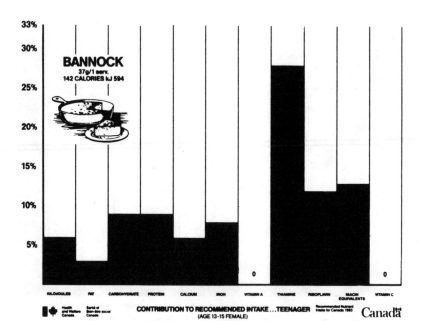

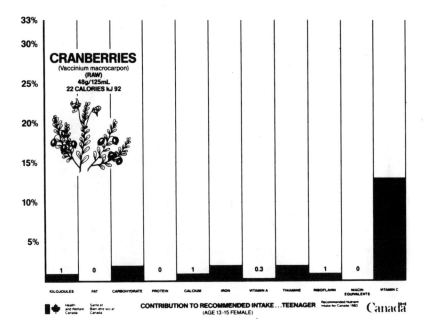

CRANBERRIES
(Vaccinium macrocarpon)
(RAW)
48g/125mL
22 CALORIES kJ 92

KILOJOULES	FAT	CARBOHYDRATE	PROTEIN	CALCIUM	IRON	VITAMIN A	THIAMINE	RIBOFLAVIN	NIACIN EQUIVALENTS	VITAMIN C
1	0		0	1		0.3		1	0	

Health and Welfare Canada   Santé et Bien-être social Canada

CONTRIBUTION TO RECOMMENDED INTAKE...TEENAGER
(AGE 13-15 FEMALE)

Recommended Nutrient Intake for Canada 1983

Canadä

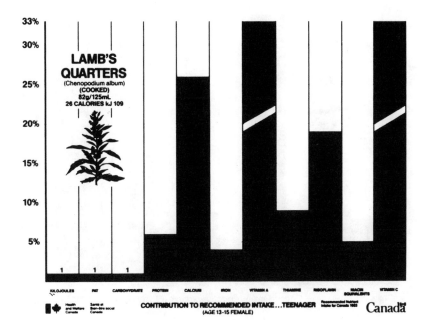

LAMB'S QUARTERS
(Chenopodium album)
(COOKED)
82g/125mL
26 CALORIES kJ 109

KILOJOULES	FAT	CARBOHYDRATE	PROTEIN	CALCIUM	IRON	VITAMIN A	THIAMINE	RIBOFLAVIN	NIACIN EQUIVALENTS	VITAMIN C
1	1	1								

Health and Welfare Canada   Santé et Bien-être social Canada

CONTRIBUTION TO RECOMMENDED INTAKE...TEENAGER
(AGE 13-15 FEMALE)

Recommended Nutrient Intake for Canada 1983

Canadä

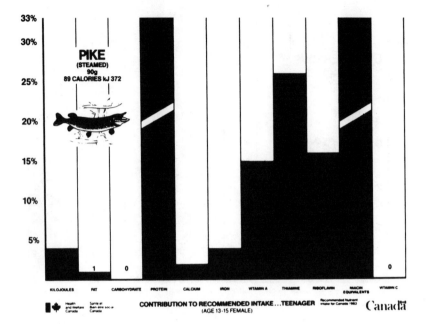

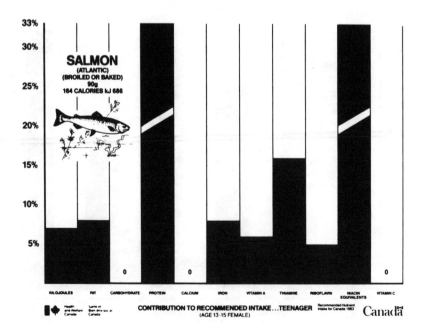

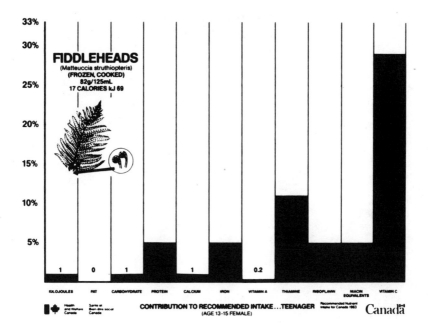

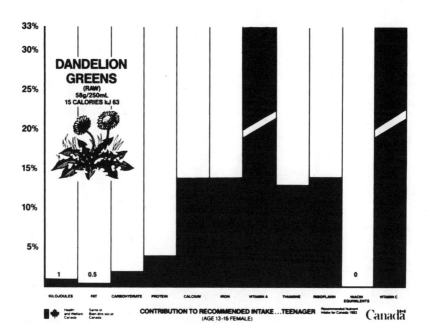

INDEX

A

B

C

D

R

S

T

V

W

Z